REFLECTIONS ON THE GOSPELS
VOLUME TWO

Reflections on the Gospels

Volume Two

*Daily Devotions for
Radical Christian Living*

John Michael Talbot

SERVANT BOOKS
Ann Arbor, Michigan

Cover photograph by Edd Anthony, O.F.M.
Cover design by Michael Andaloro

Published by Servant Books
P.O. Box 8617
Ann Arbor, Michigan 48107

88 89 90 91 92   10 9 8 7 6 5 4 3 2

ISBN 0-89283-349-1
Printed in the United States of America

Note to the Reader

REFLECTIONS ON THE GOSPELS is designed to help the reader meditate on a gospel passage throughout the day. Some readers will be particularly interested to note that the readings correspond to the daily gospel readings for the liturgical year. This second volume of *Reflections on the Gospels* covers the seventh week through the twenty-first week of Ordinary Time; an earlier volume begins with the twenty-second week and continues through the Advent and Christmas seasons. The particular week and day of the readings in this volume are indicated at the beginning of each. For example, (7:Monday) indicates that the reading is the gospel text for Monday of the seventh week in Ordinary Time. Thus, *Reflections on the Gospels* can be read in concert with the liturgical season. Whether or not you read it in this way, it is designed to bring you into contact every day with the living word of God.

On Fire for God!
Mark 9:14-29 (7:Monday)

Everything is possible to a man who trusts. . . . This kind you can drive out only by prayer (and fasting). (v. 29)

There are many "demons" to be cast out of our modern world: the constant threat of nuclear holocaust, the ever-present reality of world hunger and poverty, political unrest and war on most of our continents, and, of course, the yearly holocaust of over a million human beings, whose lives are snuffed out before they are even born. These all work against the just plan of God in our world.

No doubt the time has come for us to raise our voices for God. God has placed us in this moment of time for a reason. The reason is clear: We are to be a leaven in the dough of the world. Without the presence of those who stand against the demons in the name of God, the dough of the world will fall flat.

Never before have we faced such crises, and never before have our choices meant so much. The middle ground is fast disappearing. We are either for life or for death, for peace or for war, for justice or for oppression. As we march forward in time, it becomes increasingly apparent that we are for Christ—or, yes, for Antichrist.

Pope Paul VI said, "Peace is possible. Therefore, it is a duty." Jesus says, "Everything is possible to a man who trusts." We must remain hopeful and positive! "Greater is he who is in me than he who is in the world," says the song of Scripture. With God all things are possible! The demons of our modern world might be strong, but they can be cast out.

This is certainly true on a spiritual and eternal plane. But it is also true on the practical level. The church is truly a sleeping giant in the world. Standing alone we are weak and prone to defeat, but standing together as a people of God we are strong!

One of the keys to world peace is to solve the problem of poverty in the third world. And one of the keys to the poverty of the third world is in the materialistic countries of the West. The key to raising the spiritual consciousness of the West is to awaken this great sleeping giant called the church.

The key to waking up the church is in the parish and in awakening our own human soul! We cannot bring peace to the outer world if we do not first know inner peace. We cannot feed the hungry if we have not first been spiritually fed by the Bread of Life. We cannot bring justice if we have not yet personally experienced the justification of Christ.

This means we must be on fire for God! If we are to stop the demonic fire of the various holocausts of our modern world, the fire of God's love must burn in the depths of our souls. If we are to stop the destructive fires of the modern world, we must first deal with the fire of personal sin in our own souls.

To be effective Christian activists we must first be a people of deep and personal prayer. We cannot act if we do not pray! We cannot deeply care if we do not first experience God's care for us in personal prayer. Our souls must be consumed by God's fire. This fire does not destroy; it is a fire that saves!

Do we take time to pray before we act? Do we try to cast out the demons of our modern world by purely human strength, or do we really trust in the power of God? As we face the challenges of the future, we must radically turn to God or we will be lost. Only in him can we and our world truly be saved.

The challenge is daily. Have we really turned to Christ this day? There is always room for growth. An appropriate prayer for us today comes right from our gospel: "I do believe! Lord, help my unbelief." □

Are We Childlike?
Mark 9:30-37 (7:Tuesday)

If anyone wishes to rank first, he must remain the last one of all and the servant of all. (v. 35)

Today the attitude of childlikeness comes to mind. The gospel tells us to become the smallest if we want to be the greatest. Likewise, it tells us to recognize Jesus himself in the presence, not of some great person, but of a child.

Today's gospel speaks of children, but in reference to welcoming others: "Whoever welcomes a child such as this for my sake welcomes me." In Mark's economy of words, this Scripture jumps from a suggested attitude of personal childlikeness to an admonition to welcome children. Yet it makes much sense, especially in light of the other synoptic Gospels.

In Matthew's Gospel, Jesus says in reference to our work with the poor, "I assure you, as often as you did it for one of my least brothers, you did it for me." Thus Jesus calls us not only to a humble and childlike openness to God, but to an openness to the poor. So often they are repulsive to us, a reminder of the deficiencies of our society, of the ever-present possibility of our own material failure, or, worse yet, of the poverty of our own soul. But if we are to be really childlike we must be open to the poor. It is the demand of today's gospel. If we are open to God, we must be open to people.

This gospel also calls us to serve others. We are to seek to be "last," to be "the servant of all." If we are children, we will be servants. This too is foolishness. As Paul says, "God has put us apostles at the end of the line. . . . We are fools on Christ's account. Ah, but in Christ you are wise! We are the weak ones. You are strong! They honor you, while they sneer at us!"

Are we really childlike? Are we open to the full action of the Spirit in our life? Are we willing to work with the scandal of poverty by working with the poor? Are we willing to become least so others might be great? If we think we have passed beyond such childlikeness, then we are merely childish. If we have not yet reached the attitude of a child, then we are not yet wise. □

Different Yet United
Mark 9:38-40 (7:Wednesday)

"We tried to stop him because he was not of our company". . . "do not try to stop him. . . . Anyone who is not against us is with us." (v. 38-40)

Today's gospel speaks to me of Christian ecumenism, or the work for unity among the churches who profess the name of Jesus. Now, Jesus did personally choose the twelve apostles, and it was primarily to them that he gave the "power of the keys" of Matthew 18 and the "great commission" of Matthew 28. In the gospel accounts the work of Jesus and his band of apostles always remains the primary focus. Jesus also "appointed a further seventy-two" disciples who helped him and his apostles in his ministry. Likewise, a "great multitude" followed him about the countryside.

The history of the church shows that the authentic establishment of local communities was a work of the Holy Spirit through the apostles. The local elders, or bishops, were raised up by the Holy Spirit but were appointed or confirmed by the apostles. His apostolic succession was the visible link with the historic Jesus, for Jesus had personally chosen and empowered the apostles with the Spirit. This is the apostolic foundation of the church.

Today's account keeps us from being too narrow in our interpretation of the treasure of "apostolic succession." Jesus might have chosen the twelve, but he also rebuked them when they tried to be too exclusive about the apostolic "company." All through history, in our zeal for orthodoxy, Catholics and other Christians alike have been overly exclusive about those not of their company. Church has fought church, families have been split, towns and villages have divided, and entire nations have even gone to war—all in Jesus' name. This is a tragic scandal which deeply mars the complexion of the "spotless bride of Christ" and destroys much of our witness for Christ to the world. True, orthodoxy and truth must be maintained by the leaders who have this apostolic authority, and sometimes "it was from our ranks that they [antichrists] took their leave. . . . If they belonged to us, they would have stayed with us," as John says. But this truth is a truth that ideally unites in love; only rarely and with much sadness should it ever divide. This is, I believe, the attitude and intent of Vatican II's teaching of ecumenism.

The Scripture could also apply to ecumenism within a particular faith community. So often one group will stand off from another with an almost unspoken exclusivity. We think that, because the Holy Spirit has moved a certain way within our life and our community, he must move that way in another's experience. But this is not the case. As Paul says, "There are different gifts but the same Spirit; there are different ministries but the same Lord; there are different works but the same God who accomplishes all of them in everyone."

Throughout history the Spirit has raised up different communities within the church. There are different liturgical rites and different religious and lay orders. There are Chaldeans, Byzantines, and Romans; there are Benedictines, Franciscans, and Dominicans, just to name a few. Today there is the Cursillo movement and the charismatic renewal. Each is different, but each is similar in that it is raised up by the Spirit.

The scandal is that sometimes these groups actually compete with rather than complement one another. Deep down, some of their members really believe God works more truly in their particular group than he does in another. This might be true for the member personally, but it is rarely true when speaking of the whole church. Paul says, "Let there be no factions; rather, be united in mind and judgment.... this is what I mean: One of you will say, 'I belong to Paul,' another, 'I belong to Apollos,' still another, 'Cephas has my allegiance,' and the fourth, 'I belong to Christ.' Has Christ, then, been divided into parts?"

How do we respond to those who differ with us regarding Jesus? Do we try to stop them, or do we allow them to carry on? Which is really in keeping with the words of Christ in today's gospel? We must conserve orthodoxy, but we must always do so in love. As St. Paul finally said after many church battles, "It is true, some preach Christ from motives of envy and rivalry.... What of it? All that matters is that ... Christ is being proclaimed."

In some public matters affecting the unity of the church, we might say, "If anyone wants to argue about this, remember that neither we nor the churches of God recognize any other usage." But in other matters Paul simply said, "If you see it another way, God will clarify the difficulty for you." In the end, our position should be to simply "profess the truth in love." Then will both our unity and our diversity proclaim Jesus Christ as Lord! □

Against False Teaching
Mark 9:41-50 (7:Thursday)

It would be better if anyone who leads astray one of these simple believers were to be plunged in the sea with a great millstone fastened around his neck. If your hand is your difficulty, cut it off! (v. 42-43)

Today we move from an attitude of proper tolerance regarding Christian ecumenism to a sober warning regarding correct teaching within the church. Our beliefs affect our life-style, so it is correct to say right belief effects right practice whereas wrong belief brings forth wrong practice. This wrong practice brings pain, hurt, and even death into simple believers' lives. As St. Paul and St. James would say together, "Sin brings forth death."

This is why Paul fought so tirelessly against the wrong beliefs about Jesus that crept into the early faith communities. He said, "Warn certain people there against teaching false doctrines which promote idle speculations rather than that training in faith which God requires." Again, "Whoever teaches in any other way, not holding to the sound doctrines of our Lord Jesus Christ and the teaching of proper and true religion, should be recognized as both conceited and ignorant, a sick man in his passion for polemics and controversy." He said clearly to the Galatians, "If anyone preaches a gospel to you other than the one you received, let a curse be upon him!"

These unorthodox teachings went against the holy Scriptures and the gospel of Jesus Christ, as brought to the church and the world through the traditional teachings of the apostles. These teachings divided local churches, and they brought sin into the personal lives of sincere believers. This sin brought potential death to the church and to the people of the church. Such teaching had to be gently, lovingly, but nonetheless strongly stopped. It was a matter of life and death!

This is why James said, "Not many of you should become teachers, my brothers; you should realize that those of us who do so will be called into stricter account." Our teaching affects the real lives of real, living people. If our teaching is not in line with the teaching of Jesus and the tradition of the apostles, it does not really bring "abundant life"—it kills. This is why Paul said regarding the basic Christian teaching on sexual morality, "Let no one deceive you through worthless arguments. These are sins that bring God's wrath down on the disobedient; therefore, have nothing to do with them."

Is the church today any different? I do not think so. The same problems face the church of the twentieth century as faced the church of the first, second, and third centuries. The basic character of people has not changed all that much, so the basic problems have not changed either. Today, as then, we have well-meaning teachers trying to justify sin in order to relieve the world of sin. Today, as then, this approach is wrong. It does not really solve the problem of sin; it only adds to it. Therefore, it eventually kills the spiritual life of simple believers. Today, as then, we have well-meaning theologians who speculate about a God they do not yet personally know. Today, as then, this speculation does nothing to build the faith of the church; it only divides the church. Again, the simple believer suffers.

Paul described a problem then that is still relevant today: "They make a pretense of religion but negate its power, . . . always learning but never able to reach a knowledge of the truth." What is this "power"? It is the Holy Spirit! Today let us ask the Holy Spirit to come into our life to "lead us into all truth." Let us ask him to empower us to overcome our imprisonment to sin. Then we and our theologians can speak of a God we know personally! □

Jesus Calls Us Higher
Mark 10:1-12 (7:Friday)

"Whoever divorces his wife and marries another commits adultery against her; and the woman who divorces her husband and marries another commits adultery." (v. 11-12)

These are hard sayings for modern ears! In our culture 50 percent of all marriages end in divorce. This percentage does not change among nominal Christians. It gets a little better among regular churchgoers, but even there one out of every three marriages ends in divorce. These words of Jesus simply do not wash with the actual experience of modern life.

Actually, they did not wash with the experience of the Jews either. "Because of your stubbornness," said Jesus, "Moses permitted divorce." Furthermore, polygamy was accepted even among such faithful servants as David. Both divorce and polygamy were common practices among the primitive tribes of all cultures and religions. Today's modern culture and religion are really no exception.

The teachings of Jesus Christ lift us up to a higher level. Christian morality is not just a "baptism" of natural morality and conscience. It raises itself up higher.

This is true in many areas. In the world, sexuality is permissive; now Jesus calls us up higher, through strict monogamous and celibate chastity. In the world, the accumulation of earthly possessions is accepted; now Jesus calls us up higher, through gospel poverty. In the world, anger and revenge are accepted; now Jesus calls us up higher, through peaceful compassion, understanding, and forgiveness. Granted, Jesus' moral teachings fit squarely into the developing wisdom tradition of the Jewish sages, but they always called his disciples on to a purer and more lofty ideal.

This ideal is, quite frankly, unlivable. Even our good nature at its best does not strive for and attain such lofty ideals. It settles for something comfortably good, but it does not allow itself to become uncomfortable so as to attain the better.

For the Christian, the attainment of this better way is only possible through the empowerment of the Holy Spirit. It is not enough just to believe in Jesus. "Even the demons believe and tremble," says St. James. It is not enough to desire to be a disciple. Even the disciples did not have sufficient power to go forth and establish Jesus' church after the resurrection and ascension. "Remain here in the city until you are clothed with power from on high," said Jesus. This empowerment occurred with the giving of the Holy Spirit at Pentecost. To effectively live the Christian life as a church was impossible until then.

I would conclude by a return to statistics. Fifty percent of all modern marriages end in divorce, Christian and non-Christian alike. One out of every three churchgoing Christian marriages ends in divorce. But when a couple intentionally chooses to set aside time for prayer together every day, the statistic drops to one out of every eleven hundred! It is prayer that stirs up the commitment of the Christian couple and calls down the power of the Spirit. Even a nonreligious person has to admit, these are pretty good odds! You can bet on the Holy Spirit to empower us if we take the time to ask for daily empowerment.

Do we really seek a daily Pentecostal outpouring of the Holy Spirit in our Christian life? Do we allow the hard sayings of Jesus to make us uncomfortable enough to rise to the challenge of the better way, or do we settle only for the good in our desire for comfort? Jesus calls us to the better. The good is no longer good enough! We must be either hot or cold for Christ. The lukewarm will be rejected by the judgment of God. It is only the Holy Spirit who will fill the lukewarm muteness of our life with "tongues of fire." Without this grace we cannot effectively and obediently follow as a disciple of Christ. □

Open to the Spirit
Mark 10:13-16 (7:Saturday)

I assure you that whoever does not accept the reign of God like a little child shall not take part in it. (v. 15)

Today the gospel calls us not only to welcome little children but to actually become children. It is one thing to reach out to the "little ones" from a place of greatness. But it is quite another to actually become a little one in order to be with them.

Isn't this, after all, what God did? In order to reach human beings he became one. Paul says, "Though he was in the form of God . . . he emptied himself and took the form of a slave, being born in the likeness of men. He was known to be of human estate."

Yet we do not become like children only to reach children. This would still be condescending and proud. We become like children in order to be found acceptable to God. It is an act of humility. Without this childlike humility we cannot really know God.

To be a child means to be totally open to the will of God. Whatever God wants of us we must be open to do. So many times we say, "God, I will do anything for you except . . ." That "except" could be anything. It could be speaking in tongues or working with the poor. It could be forgiving that certain person whom we just know God must hate. To be a child means to be open to anything God wants of us. As soon as *except* becomes a word we use with God, we have ceased to be God's little child. We have grown up and left home.

For instance, how many of us say things like "I have a great respect for the charismatic gifts, but they are not for me"? The same statement could be made of contemplative life, celibacy, marriage, work with the poor, or any dimension of life within the church. We must be totally open to any gift or any call God might have for us, or we are not like children.

This attitude of childlikeness extends to becoming a fool for Christ. As Paul would say, "If any one of you thinks he is wise in a worldly way, he had better become a fool. In that way he will really be wise, for the wisdom of this world is absurdity with God.... We are fools on Christ's account."

Granted, we are not called to personally experience all aspects of the church. As Paul says, "God has set up in the church first apostles, second prophets, third teachers, then miracle workers, healers, assistants, administrators, and those who speak in tongues. Are all apostles? Are all prophets? Are all teachers? Do all work miracles or have the gift of healing? Do all speak in tongues, all have the gift of interpretation of tongues?"

Yet Paul does tell us to seek spiritual gifts. He says, "Set your hearts on spiritual gifts," and, "I should like it if all of you spoke in tongues.... Thank God, I speak in tongues more than any of you." Paul recognizes that not all will possess all the gifts, and therefore he urges, "Set your hearts on the greater gifts, ... above all the gift of prophecy.... In the church I would rather say five intelligible words to instruct others than ten thousand words in a tongue."

Ironically, Paul concludes this section on childlike openness to the Spirit by saying, "Do not be childish in your outlook. Be like children as far as evil is concerned, but in mind be mature." Be childlike, but not childish. Be a fool regarding the wisdom of the world, but be mature in the true wisdom of God.

Are we really open to the work of the Holy Spirit in our life, or are we too proud to become God's fool? In the end only the fools will be accounted mature and wise. And what about the poor? Do we reach out to the needy in an attitude of proud self-security and smug condescension? Or are we willing to become like them in order to really love them in humility?

Only those who realize their own poverty will be found worthy of the riches of heaven. Let us be poor so we might be rich. Let us be totally open to the working of the Spirit of God. □

The Choice Is Ours
Mark 10:17-27 (8:Monday)

Go and sell what you have and give to the poor; you will then have treasure in heaven. After that, come and follow me. (v. 21)

So often we hear that we are to come to Jesus "just as we are." We are to come to him with all the "possessions" of our sins and failings, trusting that he will help us to be finally divested of their weighty burden. This is true, and it brings out the fundamental doctrine of grace. As Paul says, "For it is by grace you have been saved, through faith—and this not from yourselves, it is the gift of God—not by works, so that no one can boast."

Today's gospel brings out the importance of our human choice and effort in responding to the divine call. The core of Jesus' preaching was "Repent, for the reign of God is at hand." The word *repent,* means "to convert, to change, to turn around." This implies an act of the human will. It requires action and choice. As Sirach says, "When God, in the beginning, created man, he made him subject to his own free choice. If you choose you can keep the commandments. . . . Before man are life and death, whichever he chooses shall be given him." In this mystery of faith, God requires a human response to his divine gift. It is by grace that the gift is offered, but it takes both choice and effort to reach and accept the gift. Salvation is both grace and choice, faith and works. A careful reading of St. Paul and St. James will affirm this conclusion.

But the actual demand of Jesus in today's gospel is just too high! The Jewish sages had all warned against the perils of materialism and greed, but none had dared to suggest that such total voluntary poverty was good. It was God's will that we should have abundance so we might have something to give to the poor. To wander homeless oneself was seen as an ultimate curse from

God, even by the Jewish holy men of Jesus' day: "A miserable life it is to go from house to house." One became an additional burden to society through such poverty. It made no sense!

Yet Jesus calls us to an unheard-of ideal. He calls his followers ever higher to the ideals of the new covenant kingdom of God. "The foxes have lairs, the birds of the sky have nests, but the Son of Man has nowhere to lay his head." It is foolishness, but it is the way Christ himself lived.

This ideal is not easy; it is not comfortable. The peace of this kingdom is not an external peace that requires only an inner contemplation and no external change. It is not a spiritual "feel good." Jesus' gospel requires change, and one that is radical. It requires a total renunciation of self for the sake of God and his people. It requires a total rethinking of life that changes us entirely, both inside and out! We cannot hold on to even one thing for ourselves; all must be given to God.

Paul might moderately say, "Let him work with his hands at honest labor so that he will have something to give to those in need." But he also says of the apostles, "Up to this very hour we go hungry and thirsty, poorly clad, roughly treated, wandering about homeless. We work hard at manual labor. . . . We have become the world's refuse, the scum of all." Even to those with families he says, "From now on those with wives should live as though they had none, . . . buyers should conduct themselves as though they owned nothing, and those who make use of the world as though they were not using it; for the world as we know it is passing away."

In response to this seemingly unlivable demand of Jesus, the apostles of today's gospel say, "Then who can be saved?" They must have immediately felt what we all feel when we hear these words of Jesus: shock, surprise, amazement at a demand that seems impractical and unlivable. Jesus responds, "For man it is impossible but not for God. With God all things are possible."

Jesus recognizes that this kind of external step of faith is too much for even the common religion of a human being. He knew it would take the active and extraordinary grace of God to make this drastic and radical step. As Paul says, "It is God who, in his good will toward you, begets in you any measure of desire or achievement." Jesus' words might make us uncomfortable, but the Holy Spirit is sent to us as the Comforter, the Paraclete. "I will ask the Father and he will give you another Paraclete—to be with you always." This is the essence of grace in the new covenant—the gift of the Spirit.

Jesus' words do, and should, make us externally uncomfortable. It is this uncomfortableness that will prompt us to change, to repent. But it is the giving of the Holy Spirit that strengthens and comforts us internally as we change. The gospel does not promise external peace. Its peace is internal, and it comes only in proportion to our internal and external conversion, our change, our turning to follow Jesus.

Do we seek a gospel that is comfortable or uncomfortable? Do we seek peace from externals or from the Spirit within? Are we willing to change everything in our life to conform to the way of Jesus Christ, or do we still possessively hang on to this or that as "ours"?

The challenges of our modern world offer the potential for either widespread peace or worldwide devastation. The words of Jesus require more because the cost of our choices are higher. He knew this time would come, and he knew this choice must be made. If we give up everything, he will give back more than we could ever imagine. If we become truly poor, we will become rich in God's kingdom. If we give up the "one," we will receive one-hundredfold, "both in this life and in the life to come." God wants to accomplish great things through us today, but he will not do it until we give up our human concept of the "impossible" and embrace the divine reality that Paul speaks of when he says, "I can do all things through Christ who strengthens me." Give up the one and gain the hundredfold. Do the impossible for Christ! □

Our Heavenly Hope
Mark 10:28-31 (8:Tuesday)

I give you my word, there is no one who has given up . . . for me and for the sake of the gospel who will not receive in this present age a hundred times as many . . . and persecution besides—and in the age to come, everlasting life. (v. 29-30)

Mark's version of these words are the most clear, the most promising, and the most challenging of all the Gospel accounts. He distinguishes between this age and the age to come. He is specific about the blessings but does not fail to mention the cost—persecution.

This all relates to the controversial modern topic of liberation theology. The church, in fact, supports most of the ideals of liberation theology, but it also warns against some very real dangers that lie hidden beneath its traditional Christian language. One of the biggest dangers is in making the gospel teachings about God's poor and God's people, the church, relative to a particular sociopolitical system—Marxism. In this error all of the hopes of the gospel become earthbound, tied to a system realized in this present age. Rather, various sociopolitical systems can and should surface and be supported from the perspective of the gospel and the teaching of the church.

The gospel does promise blessings for this age. We are told by Scripture and the church to work for peace and social justice by peaceful means. We are given the promise that we can achieve more than we ever dreamed possible if we will but try. Paul speaks of "him whose power now at work in us can do immeasurably more than we ask or imagine." Jesus promises "a hundred times as many" blessings for every sacrifice we make for the sake of him and his gospel. This is both hopeful and encouraging.

Jesus also promises persecution. Paul says, "Anyone who wants to live a godly life in Christ Jesus can expect to be persecuted." Sirach says, "My son, when you come to serve the Lord, prepare yourself for trials."

The history of the church has proven these texts true. The church has never fully achieved the glorious promises of Scripture but still sojourns like a pilgrim on the face of this earth. Even at times of great influence, the promises have been only partially realized. Its saints are thus not so much sociopolitical reformers as holy men and women who let God's grace overcome their personal sin. It is this personal sin that is the root of the problem of injustice in the world. People must change before systems can change.

Liberation theology errs when it makes a sociopolitical system the pivot point of the gospel and thus the fulfillment of the promises and hopes of Scripture. These promises and these hopes are totally fulfilled only in heaven. Looking for a total fulfillment on earth gives the simple believer false hopes. This will, in the end, destroy his faith, creating bitterness and despair. It will eventually work not for Christ but for Antichrist. Woe to those who lead these little ones astray!

Do we look for the fulfillment of our hope in heaven or on earth? Do we look realistically at the promises of Christ, or do we stretch them into a meaning never intended? Do we make the pivot point of the Gospels a sociopolitical revolution, or do we see Jesus and his church as the still point in a constantly changing world?

Let us fulfill the gospel admonition to work for peace and justice. Where possible, let us replace unjust structures with more just ones. But let us always remember that the only totally just government will be established at the end of the age when the Just One appears. As Scripture says, "Set all your hope on the gift to be conferred on you when Jesus Christ appears." Then we will not hope in vain.

In the end let us follow the sound advice of St. Paul: "The grace of God has appeared, offering salvation to all men. It trains us to reject godless ways and worldly desires, and live temperately, justly, and devoutly in this age as we await our blessed hope, the appearing of the glory of the great God and of our Savior Christ Jesus." If we constantly call to mind the balance and tension between this age and the age to come, we will do well. If we set our hearts on heaven, we will be effective on earth.

Today I would ask, does God want political revolutionaries, or does he want saints? Let God cleanse you of personal sin, then you might better know how to deal with the corporate sin of the sociopolitical world. But let your pivot point of reference always be Jesus and his church! Be a saint rather than a reformer. Then you will join the gentle revolution of the Spirit, which is building a kingdom that will stand throughout eternity!   □

Are You Ready to Follow?
Mark 10:32-45 (8:Wednesday)

Their mood was one of wonderment, while that of those who followed was fear. (v. 32)

It is a frightening thing to follow Jesus. His words are challenging and often sharp. They call us to a level of spirituality higher than any we have known before. To follow takes courage. It takes guts to be a Christian! We live a life of tension between the already and the not yet.

Fear is not totally unhealthy. "The beginning of wisdom is the fear of the Lord," says Scripture. Yet Scripture also says, "Love casts out all fear." What is the difference?

Healthy fear of God, awe of his greatness moves us onward, while an unhealthy fear cripples and demobilizes us. Godly fear brings healthy progress in life. The other brings death; it comes from the enemy of our soul.

The wonderment and fear of the disciples in today's gospel prompted them to mobilize, for Christ Jesus said, "Go and sell what you have and give to the poor; you will then have treasure in heaven. After that, come and follow me." The disciples had the courage to follow. They undoubtedly held high expectations for the coming Messiah. There were undoubtedly many hurdles for them to cross: giving up their families, their jobs, even their religious friends, in order to leave everything to follow Christ. Yet they did it.

James and John wanted to be "achievers" in Christ's kingdom; they wanted to be important for God. Jesus challenged them with the question, "Can you drink the cup I shall drink, or be baptized in the same bath of pain as I?" These words still sparkle with the valor and romance of "the cause."

This hot fervor of expectation and readiness to sacrifice are somehow cooled by Jesus' next words. He soberly tells them of reality: "From the cup I drink of you shall drink; the bath I am immersed in you shall share." He promises no great places of leadership or glory on earth. He only promises pain.

There is very little glamour in pain. The death Jesus eventually suffered on the cross was ordinary and tragic. He bled, he hungered, he cried out in thirst and agony. He even began to doubt—"My God, my God, why have you forsaken me?" Soldiers coming back from war do not tell of their former dreams of glory and victory. They come back as men who have seen only the bitter defeat of one side or the other, the tragic carnage of human flesh and broken human lives. Pain hurts. Death brings agony. There is little romanticism when you are in the midst of sharing the cross of Christ. There is only hurt and pain.

Are you ready for this "reality therapy" of following Jesus Christ? Sure, we need the romance of a love relationship and the promise of heavenly glory to get us through, but the human reality of intense suffering and pain will still come to the life of the average Christian—and with persecution besides! Can you take it? Jesus says, "If one of you decides to build a tower, will he not first sit down and calculate the outlay to see if he has enough money to complete his project? In the same way, none of you can be my disciple if he does not renounce all his possessions." Today, can you get past the "wonderment" and romance of the call of Christ and *really* count the cost of being a disciple? Only those who do so will withstand the eventual test. □

Shout to the Lord!
Mark 10:46-52 (8:Thursday)

Many people were scolding him to make him keep quiet, but he shouted all the louder, "Son of David, have pity on me!" (v. 48)

As with the blind beggar Bartimaeus, so it often is with us. Though the crowd professes to follow Jesus, they actually try to silence those who seek to earnestly follow the Savior. Those who recognize their blindness have nothing to lose! We call out to be saved. We realize our humiliation already. We are not afraid to be "different" in order to follow Christ.

Notice that Bartimaeus "shouted all the louder" when they tried to quiet him. So too should be our response. The Scriptures are filled with admonitions to "cry out to the Lord," to "shout," to "sing," and to "praise God loudly, with all your skill." St. Paul would encourage us, "In every place the men shall offer prayers with blameless hands held aloft." Or again, "At every opportunity pray in the Spirit, using prayers and petitions of every sort. Pray constantly." Even again, "Rejoice always, never cease praying, render constant thanks." And, "Sing praise to the Lord with all your hearts. Give thanks to God the Father always and for everything in the name of our Lord Jesus Christ."

Granted, Scripture also advises discretion in exercising such freedom. Paul says regarding the orderly exercise of the gift of tongues, "If the uninitiated or unbelievers should come in when the whole church is assembled and everyone is speaking in tongues, would they not say that you are out of your minds?" He goes on to say that prophecy is the better charismatic gift and that the use of tongues in the assembly must be accompanied by an intelligent interpretation. Even so, he concludes, "Set your hearts on prophecy, my brothers, and do not forbid those who speak in tongues, but make sure that everything is done properly and in order."

This in no way justifies those who try to quiet a free expression of praise and worship in the church. If anything, it brings out their error. They would not be wrong to insist on biblical order in the use of spiritual gifts in worship, but they themselves become unbiblical when they try to forbid their expression altogether.

Let us conclude today with a look at David. In 2 Samuel, chapter 6, David brings the ark of the covenant back to Jerusalem. "David, girt with a linen apron, came dancing before the Lord with abandon, as he and all the Israelites were bringing up the ark of the Lord with shouts of joy and the sound of the horn." David's wife, Michal, reproved him for such foolishness, for he had danced in his underclothes before the common people. David's response is significant: "I was dancing before the Lord. As the Lord lives, . . . not only will I make merry before the Lord, but I will demean myself even more. I will be lowly in your esteem, but in the esteem of the slave girls you spoke of I will be honored." And so, "Michal was childless to the day of her death."

Do we try to forbid the free expression of the Spirit in our church worship? Do we try to quiet our local Bartimaeuses and Davids? Are we ourselves afraid to be so "foolish" as to succumb to the experience of the spiritual gifts? If it is pride that keeps us back, remember Michal. She was childless, fruitless. Also remember blind Bartimaeus. He was given his sight! □

Away with Obstacles
Mark 11:11-26 (8:Friday)

He entered Jerusalem and went into the temple precincts. He inspected everything there. (v. 11)

Jesus is truly the inspector of our lives. He enters our lives even as he entered the temple of Jerusalem. As Paul says, "Are you not aware that you are the temple of God, and that the Spirit of God dwells in you?" Everything we think, feel, say, or do is "inspected" by the historical example and ongoing presence of Jesus within us. Everything rises or falls in reference to Jesus, for he is the rock in this constantly changing world.

Likewise, Jesus looks at the fruit of our life just as he looked at the fruit of the fig tree. If he finds the fruit of the Spirit, he blesses our life. If he finds our life barren, he "curses" its present course and calls us to repent, to change direction. It is not too late to change. Sirach says, "To the penitent he provides a way back." Paul says, "He wants all men to be saved and come to know the truth." In this call to change, Jesus calls us to bear much spiritual fruit.

As Paul says, "It is obvious what proceeds from the flesh: Lewd conduct, impurity, licentiousness, idolatry, sorcery, hostilities, bickering, jealousy, outbursts of rage, selfish rivalries, dissensions, factions, envy, drunkenness, orgies, and the like. I warn you, as I have warned you before: those who do such things will not inherit the kingdom of God. In contrast, the fruit of the Spirit is love, joy, peace, patient endurance, kindness, generosity, faith, mildness, and chastity. Against such there is no law!"

If we "inspect our life in Christ" we will probably find many things from the flesh still present. Jesus stops, or "curses," such things, calls us to change the directions of our life that lead to death, and empowers us by the Spirit to bear much fruit. This fruit is from the very tree of life!

Furthermore, Jesus overturns anything that perverts pure prayer in our life, for prayer is the mother of a Spirit-led life-style. The money-changers were very much a part of the recognized system of the liturgical worship of the temple. They provided the common people with the animals for sacrifice. This was supposed to be a service; it was supposed to be good. Yet this service turned in on itself, was corrupted by greed, and in the name of God perverted the will of God. Likewise, the false religion of the Revelation "was drunk with the blood of God's holy ones and the blood of those martyred for their faith in Jesus" and was "a dwelling place for demons. The kings of the earth committed fornication with her, and the world's merchants grew rich from her wealth and wantonness." Jesus overturns anything in our life that gets in the way of our prayer. He even overturns our "religion" if it is rooted in politics and economics. He does not want our spirituality to be earthbound!

Lastly, Jesus promises us that any obstacle to our genuine life of prayer and Spirit-led spirituality can be removed. There is no obstacle too large! If we walk in faith and forgiveness, we will be victorious. Faith without forgiveness is cold, yet forgiveness without faith can be directionless and without purpose. If we passively forgive people and aggressively have faith in God, the obstacles to a victorious life in Christ will be "thrown into the sea."

Are we willing to let Jesus curse the unfruitful areas of our life today? Are we willing to change so we might really bear fruit? Will we let Jesus overturn even the tables of our religious routines so that we might really pray to and have a relationship with the living God? Jesus challenges us and empowers us to do great things today! No obstacle is too big for him. We are called to faith. We are called to prayer. We are called to spiritual fruitfulness. There is nothing that should stand in our way! □

Discerning the Divine
Mark 11:27-33 (8:Saturday)

"Tell me, was John's baptism of divine origin or merely from men?" ...
"We do not know" .... *"Then neither will I tell you on what authority I do the things I do."* (v. 30, 33)

It is easy for us, with the perspective of two thousand years of Christian history, to recognize the authority of both John the Baptist and Jesus. Of course John was the forerunner of the Messiah and Jesus was the Messiah! Of course we can see that their authority was divine! We benefit from two thousand years of theological development through the great fathers of the church.

But it was not necessarily so easy to answer the question in Jesus' day. There were lots of "prophets" and "messiahs" wandering the countryside at that time. Jesus himself said, "False messiahs and false prophets will appear." John the evangelist said, "Many false prophets have appeared in the world." People went to see the newest itinerant preacher much the same way we go to a movie. It kept them occupied. It kept them "entertained." As the prophet Ezekiel says, "For them you are only a ballad singer, with a pleasant voice and a clever touch." Granted, both John the Baptist and Jesus enjoyed popularity among the religious in the land, but the crucifixion of Jesus itself shows how deep the spirituality of the average follower really was.

But what of the authority of John and Jesus and the religious symbols they employed? Is baptism found anywhere as an authoritative religious rite in the Old Testament? It was a popular sign of repentance and renewed faith among the Jews of that day. It was employed by many religious movements and itinerant preachers. But neither we nor the theologians of that day would be able to find solid evidence from the Old Testament to support its divine authority.

The authority of Jesus himself was also questionable, at the very least. The scribes and the Pharisees constantly questioned it: "How did this man get his education when he had no teacher?" Or, "Look it up. You will not find the prophet coming from Galilee." Jesus was not a priest. He was not even a schooled rabbi. Nor was his Davidic lineage clearly discernible.

As Scripture says, he was "made high priest forever according to the order of Melchizedek." This Melchizedek was a mysterious figure of Scripture. He was "without father, mother, or ancestry, without beginning of days or end of life, like the Son of God he remains a priest forever." Jesus' priesthood was "not in virtue of law expressed in a commandment concerning physical descent, but in virtue of the power of a life which cannot be destroyed."

The same could be said of the development of religious vows in the New Testament church. At first widows and virgins were enrolled. Then ascetics and penitents began to group together in houses and communities. Many men and women withdrew to the desert as hermits and then came together in monasteries. This way of life blossomed into what we now call consecrated life, which is lived by the many brothers and sisters of the hundreds of communities within the church.

It was not until the thirteenth century that the church clearly defined these vows. The only vow in the New Testament was baptism; anything more was seen as unnecessary. Are vows then invalid because they are not directly spoken of in Scripture? Furthermore, most of the early monastic founders' commitments would not qualify under what the church now calls a public vow. Was their vow any less valid before God? By whose authority did they require such a commitment of the members of their communities?

These developments were all works of the Holy Spirit. The Spirit works within the existing structures (for they too were established by the Spirit), but he often works outside and independent of those structures to remind us of his transcendence. As John says of the work of the Spirit, "You do not know where it comes from, or where it goes. So it is with everyone begotten of the Spirit." As Paul says of such a one, "The spiritual man can appraise everything, though he himself can be appraised by no one."

How do we deal with the John the Baptists of our day? How do we respond to the new forms and structures raised up by the Spirit within the church? If they are not like the ones that have come before, do we reject them? Granted, they should be tested, but not all should be rejected. As Paul says, "Test everything; retain what is good. . . . Do not stifle the Spirit." Those who so quickly reject these new forms could well have rejected the authority of John the Baptist had they lived in his day. They might too have rejected the great monastic saints of the church. Lastly, they very well could have crucified our Lord Jesus. ☐

Embrace the Cross
Mark 12:1-12 (9:Monday)

The stone rejected by the builders has become the keystone of the structure. (v. 10)

How do we deal with rejection? Oh, yes, it's easy being a Christian when all goes well. But how do we handle trials, rejection, and even failure?

Many popular preachers promise a life of prosperity and success to all followers of Jesus. They base this promise on the victory of Jesus' resurrection from the dead. "We are more than conquerors," they say. Likewise, "Greater is he who is in you than he who is in the world." Or, "By his stripes you are healed." They apply all this to the physical and emotional world, rejecting *all* sickness and anxiety as inconsistent with the Christian experience.

But the Christian experience itself reveals this promise as false. "No pupil outranks his teacher, no slave his master," says Jesus. He only promises, "If they call the head of the house Beelzebub, how much more the members of his household! . . . They will haul you into court, they will flog you in the synagogues. You will be brought to trial before rulers and kings. . . . You will be hated by all on account of me." Today's gospel parable says clearly of Jesus, "They seized and killed him and dragged him outside the vineyard." Jesus promises that they will treat us the same way.

Jesus even suffered great emotional stress. All was not peaceful and benign for him. Before the crucifixion he said, "I have a baptism to receive. What anguish I feel till it is over!" Of his agony in the garden of Gethsemane it is said, "In his anguish he prayed with all the greater intensity, and his sweat became like drops of blood." Modern doctors say he probably experienced a complete emotional breakdown. Yet he did not break faith. He did not sin.

This was also the experience of the apostles of the early church. The church is built not only upon the rejected cornerstone of Jesus Christ but also upon the completed foundation of the apostles and prophets. Paul says, "You form a building which rises on the foundation of the apostles and prophets, with Christ Jesus himself as the capstone."

How were the apostles treated? Paul says, "We are afflicted in every way possible. . . . We are persecuted but never abandoned." And, "With my many more labors and imprisonments, with far worse beatings and frequent brushes with death. Five times at the hands of the Jews I received forty lashes less one; three times I was beaten with rods; I was stoned once. . . . I traveled continually, endangered by floods, robbers, my own people, the Gentiles; imperiled in the city, in the desert, at sea, by false brothers." About emotional stress Paul says, "Full of doubts, we never despair," and, "There is that daily tension pressing in on me." Paul was not always peaceful! Yet he was not in sin.

Peter, too, speaks of enduring many sufferings for Jesus. It comes as no surprise then that both Peter and Paul ended their lives in martyrdom. Likewise, all the apostles except John are traditionally believed to have died as martyrs for their faith in Jesus, and even John is reported to have suffered exile on the island of Patmos. All ended their lives without seeing the full-blown glory of what we now so surely call the church.

What a contrast this is to both the "prosperity" evangelists and the liberation theologians! Both promise some kind of earthly guarantee of success for spiritual fidelity to Jesus Christ. One is conservative in its politics, the other is liberal. One emphasizes the private and personal, the other the civil and corporate. But both tend to miss the balanced truth of the gospel. The gospel promises an inner spiritual success that transcends both emotional and material failure. It promises certain crosses in this world, but it also promises the hope of eventual resurrection and eternal life in heaven.

Beware of false hopes; they lead to disappointment. Embrace and face the real rejections and crosses that come into your life. Do not be surprised if you experience emotional anguish and physical pain. Jesus experienced them too. Yet he made it through to resurrection. You will too if you face your troubles with Christ.

He is your only real hope. His way is the only real way past rejection and pain. □

Jesus' Way of Love
Mark 12:13-17 (9:Tuesday)

Give to Caesar what is Caesar's, but give to God what is God's. (v. 17)

Today it has become "hip" for socially conscious Christians to criticize the civil government. It is almost like a religious fad. Many of us have seen the movie *Ghandi* and are now trying to "Ghandiize" Jesus Christ. But while Ghandi had many admirable aspects to his life and teaching, he was not Jesus Christ. Nor were all his examples and teachings fully compatible with Christianity. Nor is the peace and social justice bandwagon always really Christlike in either the direction of its journey or the melody of its song. A rebellious or disobedient attitude or spirit is not fundamentally acceptable for the Christian who follows the teaching of the New Testament.

St. Peter says, "Because of the Lord, be obedient to every human institution, whether to the emperor as sovereign or to the governors he commissions for the punishment of criminals and the recognition of the upright. Such obedience is the will of God."

Paul says also, "Let everyone obey the authorities that are over him, for there is no authority except from God, and all authority that exists comes from God. As a consequence, the man who opposes authority rebels against the ordinance of God. . . . You must obey, then, not only to escape punishment but also for conscience' sake." He concludes with a restatement of Jesus' teachings concerning taxes: "You pay taxes for the same reason, magistrates being God's ministers. . . . Pay each one his due; taxes to whom taxes are due; toll to whom toll is due; respect and honor to anyone who deserves them."

The amazing thing to consider about these teachings is the government under which Christianity was born. It was the government of the Roman Empire, an orderly government but not always what we would consider just. Rome may well have prided itself on its "roman justice," but its system propagated unequal rights between slaves and free, men and women, citizens and aliens, and it suppressed any new concept of religious freedom. This government was, in fact, the civil instrument used by the Jews to kill Jesus and James, not to mention its own initiative to kill apostles such as St. Peter and St. Paul and its systematic slaughter of countless Christians in the Roman arena. Rome was a violent, bloodthirsty, and unjust government ruling a militant and aggressive people.

Yet Jesus did not resist this government with anything but love. The passive resistance and civil disobedience of Ghandi are nowhere found in the example or teachings of Jesus Christ. He teaches only the total nonresistance of the Sermon on the Mount: "What I say to you is: offer no resistance to injury. When a person strikes you on the right cheek, turn and offer him the other." He does not passively resist, he nonresists! He personally submits to unjust leaders, both religious and civil, even to the point of death. He organizes no peaceful protests. He leads no march. He is silent. He only loves. The apostles do largely the same.

It must be acknowledged that today's civil government, especially in America, is different from that of ancient Rome. As citizens we are called upon to participate in the government. There are steps we can obediently take to establish justice. We can vote. We even have the freedom to protest and march, as long as it is orderly, respectful, and peaceful. There is much we can do in a country such as ours. Isaiah does say, "Make justice your aim: redress the wronged, hear the orphans' plea, defend the widow."

Yet it seems to me that both major political parties in the United States are out of line with the traditional Christian standards of a morally just civil government. Perhaps we need to seriously consider a truly moral third option for the Christian vote? All this can be done in a humble attitude of obedience and respect within our country.

But where do we cross the line from giving our "reply in humble respect" to an attitude of disobedience and religious pride? When does our demonstration of peace and social justice cease to be really Christian? The greatest demonstration we can give is love. The greatest example we can follow is that of Jesus. Then we will follow not the way of a mere holy man or human philosopher; we will follow the way of Jesus Christ, the way of God himself! □

Let the Spirit Lead
Mark 12:18-27 (9:Wednesday)

You are badly misled, because you fail to understand the Scriptures or the power of God. . . . He is the God of the living, not of the dead. You are very much mistaken. (v. 24, 27)

Jesus spoke these words not to pagans but to religious people. He spoke them to a recognized Jewish sect called the Sadducees. They were a people strongly dedicated to God and the Jewish religion. They were, in effect, both ultra-conservatives and rationalists. If you could not find something in the Torah or the first five books of the Old Testament, the books of Moses, then they would not accept it. As these books say, "You shall not add to it what I command you nor subtract from it."

The Sadducees obeyed the letter of the law. As a result, they rejected all further divine revelation. If the Holy Spirit spoke, they refused to listen. They believed God had said all he had to say through the books of Moses. Consequently, they did not believe in the spirit world nor in the afterlife of the soul or spirit. They became rationalists: If they couldn't see it, feel it, or understand it, then they wouldn't believe it. Their extreme conservatism led them to a rationalism that literally cut them off from the power of true spiritual life! Jesus preached a doctrine of eternal life, but the Sadducees didn't even accept the concept.

When the Sadducees question Jesus in today's gospel about how many wives this man will have in the resurrection from the dead, they are not asking sincerely. They are just engaging in theological squabbling. They are playing games! All they really want to do is trap Jesus with his own words. Jesus responds clearly and directly. He will not play their game, yet by not playing he plays better than they do. He simply reaffirms the reality of the resurrection. He responds without fear.

It is not enough for "religious" people to read the Scriptures without knowing their spiritual power. Jesus quotes the Scriptures often. He says of the law, "Whoever breaks the least significant of these commands and teaches others to do so shall be called least in the kingdom of God." But he also says, "The Spirit . . . will guide you to all truth." The Scriptures were written under the inspiration of the Spirit. If we are to know the reality of the Scriptures, we must read them under the guidance of the Holy Spirit.

St. Paul says to Timothy, "All Scripture is inspired by God and useful for teaching." But he also warns about those who "make a pretense of religion but negate its power, . . . always learning but never able to reach a knowledge of the truth."

And where do we stand today? Do we read Scripture like a textbook or like a prayer book? It is not enough to study it scientifically. It must be prayed. It must be studied prayerfully under the guidance of the Spirit. St. Bonaventure said you could study Scripture all your life and still never know God. We must "bow humbly under God's mighty hand" and admit the frailty of our understanding. We must seek the guidance of the Spirit through prayer if we are to properly study the Scriptures, which were inspired by the Spirit.

Today let us read the Scriptures as a prayer, as a personal love letter from God. When we read them in this way, all becomes simple and clear. In this approach even the profound mysteries of the faith become accessible to the merest children. This might offend some scholars, but after all, this is the very reason why we have Scripture. It opens the kingdom of God to children and requires even the learned to become as children. Otherwise they will not understand. Let us seek the power of God as we read the Scriptures. Let us pray that Jesus never says to us, "You are very much mistaken." □

The Heart of the Law
Mark 12:18-34 (9:Thursday)

You shall love your neighbor as yourself. . . . You are not far from the reign of God. (v. 31, 34)

Jesus was frequently questioned by the scribes and Pharisees. They were always ready to debate, to argue about the fine points of doctrine and religion. Jesus replied with some of his harshest words to the "religious" of his day: "Frauds," "blind guides," "blind fools," "hypocrites," "brood of vipers." "You pay tithes on mint and herbs and seeds while neglecting the weightier matters of the law, justice and mercy and good faith." These are among Jesus' descriptions of the scribes and Pharisees of his day.

The Pharisees were different from the Sadducees of yesterday's gospel. They were the progressives, the "spiritual sect" of the Jews. Doctrinally they believed most of the things that Jesus taught: eternal life, the reality of the spirit world, the wisdom teaching of the Jewish sages. But they still became trapped in legalism. They still lost the spirit with their emphasis on the law. They started off well enough, but they were sidetracked by an overemphasis on externals.

The scribes too had begun as a good sect. The Scripture says, "The scribe's profession increases his wisdom. . . . His care is to seek the Lord, his Maker, to petition the Most High. . . . Then, if it pleases the Lord Almighty, he will be filled with a spirit of understanding." The scribe could potentially be a humble and earnest seeker of the will of God.

Today's good scribe does not come to debate; he comes to seek. With the "reborn" Nicodemus and the good Joseph of Arimathea, he comes with an open heart to seek the heart of God's word. He knows that to love God and love neighbor "is worth more than any burnt offering or sacrifice."

Jesus teaches that we must fulfill the law but must not harden our heart to the law's heart, the heart of God. Otherwise we do not understand the heart, the purpose, of God's law. "Do not think that I have come to abolish the law and the prophets. I have come, not to abolish them, but to fulfill them," says Jesus. But he also taught in accordance with that law that "the heart of the law is mercy."

St. Paul also knew about those who loved to argue about religion while missing the heart of God. He warns against those who have a "passion for polemics and controversies. From these come envy, dissension, slander, evil suspicions—in a word, the bickering of men with twisted minds who have lost all sense of the truth." He encourages Timothy to charge his church to "stop disputing about mere words. This does no good and can be the ruin of those who listen." This syndrome of religious argument is nothing new to the people of God!

Such argumentation does little to unite; it tends to divide. That is why true love of God requires love of neighbor. We can argue about the fine points of ritual and liturgy and still be far from a love that unites us with God and neighbor.

James speaks of a further relationship between our words and our love of God and neighbor. He says, "The tongue . . . is a restless evil, full of deadly poison. We use it to say, 'Praised be the Lord and Father'; then use it to curse men, though they are made in the likeness of God. . . . This ought not be so."

In today's gospel, when the scribe sees a unifying love as more important than "burnt offerings or sacrifices," Jesus responds by saying, "You are not far from the reign of God."

How far are we from the reign of God? Are we willing to immerse ourselves in liturgy and theology but unwilling to really love our brothers and sisters? Does our study of Scripture and theology really bring us into a love relationship with God, or does it only teach us about God? Today we have a choice: We can be like the scribes who studied the law yet were still condemned by Jesus or we can be like the humble scribe who sought the heart of God's law. It is the scribe of the latter sort that Jesus loved.   □

Beyond Human Wisdom
Mark 12:35-37 (9:Friday)

How can the scribes claim, "The Messiah is David's son"? . . . If David himself addresses him as "Lord," in what sense can he be his son? (v. 35, 37)

Time and again we see that a merely human and even theological reading of Scripture is simply not enough. The religious leaders of Jesus' day were serious theologians. They devoted themselves to the study of the law and the sayings of the sages. Yet they still missed the real meaning of the Scripture.

Paul attests to his theological training as a Pharisee when he says, "I sat at the feet of Gamaliel and was educated strictly in the law of our fathers." As Sirach says, "Frequent the company of the elders; let your feet wear away his doorstep! Reflect on the precepts of the Lord, let his commandments be your constant meditation." Why then was the theological training of the Jewish religious leaders unable to prepare them for the coming of the Messiah in Jesus of Nazareth? Paul says, "I can testify that they are zealous for God though their zeal is unenlightened."

First, it must be admitted that from a purely human approach to theology, some of the Pharisees' interpretations of the prophets seem more rational and sound than those of the first Christians, which seem to stretch the original intent of the prophet beyond the situation to which he had spoken. For example, the Christian interpretation of Isaiah's "The virgin shall be with child and give birth to a son, and they shall call him Emmanuel" is more safely understood as a prophecy about Hezekiah, son of Ahaz. This is true especially in light of the fact that the word *virgin* is safely interpreted "young maiden."

Jesus himself did not teach according to what he learned from human teachers: "My doctrine is not my own; it comes from him who sent me." Concerning the Jews' unbelief he said, "Neither do you have his [the Father's] abiding in your hearts because you do not believe the One he has sent." The Jews asked, "How did this man get his education when he had no teachers?" Jesus knew the Scriptures, but he did not fit into any theological school, because he taught according to the Spirit of God, not according to the limited wisdom of men. He was not only able to perceive more clearly than his contemporaries the main emphasis of Scripture, but he was also able to discern the subtle prejudices of the rabbinical interpretations. Jesus' view was clear and fresh. The humanly safer and more rational interpretation of Scripture came to the aid of the Jewish theologians more often than to Jesus and the first Christians.

It must be remembered that the traditional Christian interpretation of the Old Testament goes back through the apostles to Jesus himself. Luke says that after Jesus' resurrection he personally took the apostles through the entire Old Testament! "Beginning, then, with Moses and all the prophets, he interpreted for them every passage of Scripture which referred to him." Thus, apostolic tradition concerning Scripture is directly linked to the personal interpretation of Jesus.

Furthermore, we have also been given the Spirit. As Jesus promised, "Being the Spirit of truth he will guide you to all truth." The Spirit will speak through us when we are questioned: "The Spirit of your Father will be speaking in you." It was this Spirit who enabled Peter to recognize Jesus as the Messiah; "No mere man has revealed this to you, but my heavenly Father." Likewise, we must be empowered by the Spirit before we can effectively give witness to Jesus as the Christ. "You will receive power when the Holy Spirit comes down on you; then you are to be my witnesses."

Therefore, it is the Spirit working through the apostolic tradition and witness of the church that enables us to perceive the truth of Jesus. Without the Spirit we cannot really understand the Scriptures. Oh, yes, we might have a human theological wisdom, but our enlightenment will not be divine. As Paul says, "God has revealed this wisdom to us through the Spirit. . . . We speak not in words of human wisdom but in words taught by the Spirit."

Do we seek the enlightenment of the Spirit before we read the Scriptures? If we disagree with the apostolic tradition of the church, do we do so because of the Spirit or because of mere human wisdom? Do we always seek the conservative and the "safe," thus running the risk of stifling the Spirit? Let us not just study God's word. It is a word that must be prayed. Then the Spirit will guide us, and the whole church, to all wisdom and truth. □

Give Till It Hurts
Mark 12:38-44 (9:Saturday)

They gave from their surplus wealth, but she gave from her want, all that she had to live on. (v. 44)

Here again we come face-to-face with Jesus' call to a love and charity that is at once both heartwarming and demanding. The story of the widow's mite has stirred hearts for two thousand years. It has reminded us of the elderly and widowed of our churches. They are faithful to the seemingly small things of the church, but in essence they are the backbone of the faith community. Yes, this story warms our heart.

But it should also make us squirm. Jesus has challenged the very life-style of most of his listeners; he certainly challenges the life-style of most of us in the Christian West! He calls us to give not only when convenient and comfortable but even when the giving of a gift is hard!

It is this kind of giving that Jesus himself practiced. Was it easy for the Creator of the universe to take on flesh and become subject to the elements as a man? Paul says, "He emptied himself and took the form of a slave, being born in the likeness of men." Slaves have nothing for themselves; they serve another.

The self-emptying didn't stop there: "He was known to be of human estate, and it was thus that he humbled himself, obediently accepting even death, death on a cross!" Jesus' self-emptying, his "slavery," led him to give to the point of actual death—completely giving up not only his "wants" but also his "means" in order to save another. He gave up his very life in his giving.

But how are we supposed to keep helping the hurting if we ourselves lose the means by which we help? If a man jumps into the deep water to save a drowning person, he better know how to swim himself, or surely they both will drown. Paul says, "The willingness to give should accord with one's means, not go beyond them. The relief of others ought not to impoverish you; there should be a certain equality. Your plenty at the present time should supply their need so that their surplus may one day supply your need, with equality as the result." Here Paul has to take the radical and challenging words of Jesus and apply them on a practical level to the local church of Corinth. This allows relief of the poor to become "development," so they might actually help themselves.

Many people use this Scripture to justify their many possessions. They say they need their many things in order to be "whole." But I must say that even this practical approach leaves us with an awesome challenge. How often do we really see the "equality" Paul recommends among our local churches? More times than not our rich still live luxuriously while our poor are in want of even the basics of life—food, clothing, housing, medical assistance. This equality certainly does not exist on a national level, as the inner city and rural poor of our church clearly do not live equally with our rich. Even more clearly, this "practical" equality does not exist globally. Our third world church is often in actual destitution, while we of the West continue to satisfy our every want, depriving our brothers and sisters of what they really need.

Do we live up to even the practical application of Jesus' awesome challenge? Are we willing to let Jesus' words make us feel all warm and bubbly, but unwilling to let them shake us from our comfortable life-style? Let's not rationalize Jesus' call on our life. Let's not accept the call to loving comfort without the call to love's sacrifice. Let's sacrifice our wants and give to the needy. Then we will find out how little we actually need. Then will the members of the church be truly equal. Better yet, let's go beyond and give from our actual means so that others might live. Then will we sacrifice and give with the love of Jesus.   □

Undying Love
Matthew 5:1-12 (10:Monday)

When he saw the crowds he went up on the mountainside. After he had sat down his disciples gathered around him, and he began to teach them: "How blest . . . " (v. 1-3)

Today we enter into the very heart of Jesus' teachings. What the Ten Commandments are to the entire Old Testament law, so the Beatitudes are to Jesus' teachings in the New Testament. We can study these alone and come to know all the rest. They show the very heart of Jesus Christ.

Notice that Jesus goes up in response to the crowd. His teaching is in response to their need. Jesus says, "Come to me, all you who . . . find life burdensome, and I will refresh you. . . . I am gentle and humble of heart." He also says, "It is mercy I desire and not sacrifice. I have come to call not the self-righteous but sinners."

The Sermon on the Mount with the Beatitudes calls the multitude, but it calls us with love. The Beatitudes fall in with the tradition of the Jewish wisdom literature of Proverbs, Ecclesiasticus, Sirach, and Wisdom. But they go far beyond these with their new ideal of unconditional love. They call us to a morality higher than any other in the world. They motivate with love, not with fear.

The Old Testament says, "The beginning of wisdom is the fear of the Lord." But the New Testament says, "Love casts out all fear." Jesus says to the sinner, "Come to me. . . . I will refresh you."

The Beatitudes show Jesus' unfailing love for the crowd. "Blest are the poor in spirit. . . . Blest too are the sorrowing. . . . Blest are the lowly, . . . they who hunger and thirst for holiness, . . . they who show mercy, . . . the single-hearted, . . . the peacemakers, . . . those persecuted for holiness' sake." Jesus looked upon the crowds, the masses of simple people, and "his heart was moved with pity."

Here one sees the heart of his words, "I have come to call not the self-righteous but sinners." He does not support sin, but he unconditionally loves the sinner. He knew their life; he knew their longings. Jesus said to the woman caught in adultery, "I do not condemn you. You may go. But from now on, avoid this sin." Jesus strongly preached penance: "Reform your lives! The kingdom of heaven is at hand." But he did this with an irresistible call and challenge of love.

St. Paul has often been accused of not fully understanding the liberating love of Jesus. But he has written the most classical "love scripture" in all the Bible outside of the words of Jesus himself. Ponder these words: "Love is patient; love is kind. Love is not jealous, it does not put on airs, it is not snobbish. Love is never rude, it is not self-seeking, it is not prone to anger; neither does it brood over injuries. Love does not rejoice in what is wrong but rejoices with the truth. There is no limit to love's forbearance, to its trust, its hope, its power to endure. Love never fails." If we could fulfill these words alone, we would totally change our life and the world for Christ!

In today's church there is so much emphasis on spiritual, doctrinal, and social issues. The issues are usually good and worthy of discernment, but sometimes the issues of the people of the church become more important than God's simple love. Here we actually miss God by an overzealous service in and to the church!

Do we sometimes become hard-hearted and unapproachable while we crusade with our issues? Do we miss the Giver by getting sidetracked in the gifts? Do we miss God by worshiping God's truth? Gifts should lead us to the Giver. Truth should lead us to God. But if we find God, we should also find a true and heartfelt love. "God is love," says the beloved disciple. □

Anointed to Shine
Matthew 5:13-16 (10:Tuesday)

You are the light of the world. A city set on a hill cannot be hidden. . . . In the same way, your light must shine before men so that they may see goodness in your acts and give praise to your heavenly Father. (v. 14, 16)

In the Acts of the Apostles Peter describes Jesus: "He went about doing good works and healing all who were in the grip of the devil, and God was with him." Jesus too was called to let the light of his good works shine before all. As the prophet Isaiah says, "I will make you a light to the nations, that my salvation may reach to the ends of the earth."

To be a Christian means to be "like Christ"—that is the meaning of the word. The word *Christ* means "anointed one." But anointed by whom and by what? Anointed by God the Father with God the Spirit. At Jesus' baptism John the Baptist "saw the Spirit of God descend like a dove and hover over him. With that, a voice from the heavens said, 'This is my beloved Son. My favor rests on him.'" As Jesus himself said at the beginning of his public ministry, "The spirit of the Lord is upon me; therefore, he has anointed me."

Christians are called to be anointed by the Spirit! This anointing brings spiritual power to their works. Jesus told the apostles to wait for the anointing of the Spirit before beginning their ministry: "Remain here in the city until you are clothed with power from on high." After Pentecost the apostles went forth with power: "Many wonders and signs were peformed by the apostles." We too must be anointed by the Spirit if our "good works" are to really "shine before men."

This anointing is not something that happens once and then is automatically with us forever. Yes, we might be anointed by the Spirit in the sacraments of Baptism and Confirmation. Yes, we might receive the "baptism of the Spirit" at a prayer meeting. But neither of these valid gifts from God nullify the need for daily conversion and spiritual baptism.

St. Paul urges Timothy to "stir into flame the gift of God bestowed when my hands were laid upon you. The Spirit God has given us is no cowardly spirit." Jesus says, "Whoever wishes to be my follower must deny his very self, take up his cross *each day,* and follow in my steps." St. Bernard speaks of this daily conversion: "You cannot stand still. . . . You go up, you go down; if you try to stay, you are ruined."

Are we willing to actively strive after the anointing of the Spirit today? Paul says, "Set your hearts on spiritual gifts," the gifts of the Spirit. Jesus says, "Seek and you shall find." If we do not seek we will not find. Are we ready to get busy and seek today? If our "words" have no power, it is because they are not anointed. If they are not anointed, it is because we have not asked. Ask for the Spirit's anointing today. Stir up the gifts. Let your light shine before all the world.   □

Scripture Brings Life
Matthew 5:17-19 (10:Wednesday)

Do not think I have come to abolish the law and the prophets. I have come, not to abolish them, but to fulfill them. (v. 17)

Jesus was a good Jew. He was not a rebel. He was not an antagonist nor even a revolutionary. He was an obedient son of an ancient faith—the faith of Abraham, Moses, and the prophets.

All of Jesus' actions and teachings were based on the law. Granted, he sometimes seemed to break the law, but he always fulfilled the heart of the law, and he supported his "unorthodox" way with a solid example from Scripture.

The law, the Scriptures, is given for our good. Deuteronomy says, "Now, Israel, hear the statutes and decrees which I am teaching you to observe, that you may live." Jesus Christ, the living Word of the new covenant, said of himself, "I came that they might have life and have it to the full."

St. Paul also speaks of the good and life-giving quality of Scripture: "Everything written before our time was written for our instruction, that we might derive hope from the lessons of patience and the words of encouragement in the Scriptures." He says to his disciple Timothy, "Likewise, from your infancy you have known the sacred Scriptures, the source of the wisdom which through faith in Jesus Christ leads to salvation. All Scripture is inspired of God and is useful for teaching—for reproof, correction, and training in holiness so that the man of God may be fully competent and equipped for every good work."

But for Paul the Scripture was not just a legalistic word—it was alive in Christ and his church! Just as Jesus was a "living Word" come down from heaven to dwell among living people, so did Jesus appoint living men to be his apostles and preach his word of salvation. They were anointed by the Spirit of the living God at Pentecost and empowered to fulfill this commission. Thus it was that the living God sent a living Word to a living people through the very life of Jesus Christ and the apostles. The word is not written in stone. It is written in the very life of Christ! "He is the God of the living, not of the dead."

This is why Paul says to Timothy not only to follow the Scripture but also, "You have followed closely my teaching and my conduct. . . . You, for your part, must remain faithful to what you have learned and believed, because you know who your teachers were." The early church of Acts 2 followed not the Scripture alone. It followed "apostolic instruction." From this living apostolic tradition the Old Testament was interpreted and the New Testament itself was brought forth. You cannot take one without the other.

It is because of this living tradition that Paul was able to say, "Owe no debt to anyone except the debt that binds us to love one another. He who loves his neighbor has fulfilled the law. . . . Love never wrongs the neighbor, hence love is the fulfillment of the law."

Do we really take the time to read the Scriptures? Do we see them as oppressive laws from the past or as life-giving guidance for the future? Do we seek guidance from the written Scripture alone, or do we seek to "flesh out" the authority of Scripture within the authority of the Spirit-filled church? In our spirituality do we rebel against the authority of the church which brought forth this Scripture, or do we let both the Scriptures and the church speak to us with God-given authority? Finally, do the laws of Scripture and the church become complicated and burdensome to us, or do we retain the simplicity of love through them all? Remember, Jesus says, "You shall love the Lord your God with your whole heart, with your whole soul, and with your whole mind. . . . You shall love your neighbor as yourself. On these two commandments the whole law is based, and the prophets as well." □

Put Away Anger
Matthew 5:20-26 (10:Thursday)

If you bring your gift to the altar and there recall that your brother has anything against you, leave your gift at the altar, go first to be reconciled with your brother, and then come and offer your gift. (v. 23-24)

Jesus' teaching on forgiveness is a counterpart to his teaching on love. It is forgiveness that brings out the attitude of love. In Jesus' teaching you cannot take one without the other. Even as his teaching on love takes us a step higher than the Old Testament, so too does his teaching on forgiveness or reconciliation.

Forgiveness of others is linked to an effective prayer life. Jesus says, "When you stand to pray, forgive anyone against whom you have a grievance so that your heavenly Father may in turn forgive your faults." As Paul says to the Colossians, "Bear with one another; forgive whatever grievances you have against one another. Forgive as the Lord has forgiven you." In the Lord's Prayer do we not pray, "Forgive us our trespasses, as we forgive those who trespass against us"? Prayer without heartfelt forgiveness is a powerless, external exercise.

Paul also applies this to the celebration of the Lord's Supper. He says to the Corinthians, "Whoever eats the bread or drinks the cup of the Lord unworthily sins against the body and blood of the Lord. A man should examine himself first." This examination concerns sin in general, but Paul's line of thought draws directly from the teaching of Jesus in today's gospel. With the words of Jesus, we see the emphasis on forgiveness. So we should forgive others before we go to the altar of the Lord's table.

Forgiveness is the "defuser" of explosive anger. Today's gospel links Jesus' words on anger with his teaching on forgiveness. He says, "Everyone who grows angry with his brother shall be liable to judgment.... If you bring your gift to the altar and there recall that your brother has anything against you ..." Paul says the same thing to the Ephesians: "Get rid of all bitterness, all passion and anger, harsh words, slanders, and malice of every kind. In place of these, be kind to one another, compassionate, and mutually forgiving, just as God has forgiven you in Christ." If God forgives us, then we can forgive others. And if we forgive others, our anger will be defused.

Unrighteous anger is a sin, and sin brings death. We think it makes us feel better to get angry, but it eventually makes us feel worse. It puts our attitude and even our body into a negative spiral that ends in death. Doctors say unreconciled anger can actually cause disease that kills! As James says, "Once passion has conceived, it gives birth to sin, and when sin reaches maturity it begets death." It is much more fun to love than to be angry.

The power of forgiveness is seen in prayer for physical healing. St. James says, "This prayer uttered in faith will reclaim the one who is ill, and the Lord will restore him to health. If he has committed any sins, forgiveness will be his. Hence, declare your sins to one another, and pray for one another, that you may find healing." Anger causes sickness. The prayer for healing must include the forgiveness that defuses anger, or the prayer simply will not work.

Are we angry today? Do we carry resentments and hurts that make us bitter and angry deep inside? Do we seek miracles of healing in our prayer life? We must release and let go of our anger before our prayers will have spiritual power. The best way to do this is through mutual forgiveness, which brings healing and joy. Anger brings only death and darkness. Forgiveness is really much more fun! □

Tough Love
Matthew 5:27-32 (10:Friday)

If your right eye is your trouble, gouge it out and throw it away! (v. 29)

This is aggressive language! Jesus does not teach some kind of passive, always-feel-good, be-good-to-yourself spirituality. He teaches a spirituality that is bottom-line and real! Sometimes it gets tough to deal with the problems of life. Jesus does say, "The kingdom of God has suffered violence, and the violent take it by force."

Paul also uses violent language to describe our battle with sin: "Put to death whatever in your nature is rooted in earth:

fornication, uncleanness, passion, evil desires, and that lust which is idolatry. These are the sins which provoke God's wrath." Peter too uses aggressive language about breaking with sin: "So strip away everything vicious, everything deceitful, pretenses, jealousies, and disparaging remarks of any kind."

In a way we have a choice. Either we can get aggressive with our sins or God can. It is up to us. But rest assured that our sins will eventually be dealt with.

It is as if God were a fire. The brightness of his mystical fire will simply burn away all that is not of him. All that is darkness will be dispelled. Either we can embrace the fire or we can run from it. If we embrace it, it will become a passionate fire of divine love. If we try to run, it will become a painful fire of divine chastisement and punishment. But the fire remains the same. The choice is up to us!

As Paul says, "Everyone must be careful how he builds. . . . If different ones build on this foundation with gold, silver, precious stones, wood, hay, or straw, the work of each will be made clear. . . . Fire will test the quality of each man's work. If the building a man has raised on this foundation still stands, he will receive his recompense; if a man's building burns, he will suffer loss. He himself will be saved, but only as one fleeing through fire."

Peter also uses this analogy of fire, saying, "You may for a time have to suffer many trials; but this is so that your faith, which is more precious than the passing splendor of fire-tried gold, may by its genuineness lead to praise, glory, and honor when Jesus Christ appears."

Either God can get tough with our sin or we can. Either way it will be dealt with by the power of God.

Often we must be tough to overcome a deeply rooted sin. We have to make a clean break with our past, or our past will constantly rob us of our future in God. It's like going on a diet: sometimes the only way to control our food intake is to physically distance ourselves from opportunities of obvious temptation. As Paul says, "Make no provision for the desires of the flesh." Of making this clean break with the past he says, "Those things I used to consider gain I have now reappraised as loss in the light of Christ. . . . For his sake I have forfeited everything; I have accounted all else rubbish so that Christ may be my wealth."

Are we willing to radically break with our sinful past? Or do we try to live in two worlds? Jesus says, "You cannot serve God and money." And Elijah says, "How long will you straddle the issue?" Get in touch with your deeply rooted sins. Get aggressive with the sins that pursue you with a grip of death. Then you will be set free. Then you will be born again! □

The Taming of the Tongue
Matthew 5:33-37 (10:Saturday)

Do not swear at all. . . . Say, "Yes" when you mean "Yes" and "No" when you mean "No." Anything beyond that is from the evil one. (v. 34, 37)

How we abuse the power of the spoken word, especially in our Western society of written legal contracts. We do not often consider the spoken word all that binding. We throw words around cheaply. We flatter, we promise, we also slander and criticize. Somehow we don't consider what we say to be all that important. Our words must be written down or tape-recorded before they carry any real weight!

The words of Jesus stand in stark contrast to our Western mentality. His words speak of the importance of the spoken word. This makes sense, for Jesus was a Mideastern man. In the Mideastern culture the spoken word is extremely important. It is seen as the extension of a person's very soul. Your word is your soul! If words are abused, souls are abused. If words are taken lightly, souls are taken lightly. St. John's Gospel says that Jesus is God because he is the Word of God: "In the beginning was the Word; the Word was in God's presence, and the Word was God. . . . The Word became flesh and made his dwelling among us, and we have seen his glory: the glory of an only son coming from the Father, filled with enduring love." Jesus was the very soul of God, for Jesus was the Word of God incarnate!

The Jewish sages are forerunners to Jesus in their teaching. As the Proverbs say, "Where words are many, sin is not wanting." Sirach says, "Be consistent in your thoughts; steadfast be your words. Be swift to hear, but slow to answer. If you have the knowledge, answer your neighbor; if not, put your hand over your mouth. Honor and dishonor through talking! . . . the lips of the impious talk of what is not their concern, but the words of the prudent are carefully weighed."

St. Paul also speaks of the importance of the spoken word: "Never let evil talk pass your lips; say only the good things men need to hear, things that will really help them. . . . Nor should there be any obscene, silly, or suggestive talk; all that is out of place."

Words not only express our own soul; they affect the life, the soul, of those to whom we speak. That is why we should say only "the good things people really need to hear." Paul goes on, "Get rid of all harsh words and slander." As Sirach says, "A blow from the tongue smashes bones; many have fallen by the edge of the sword, but not as many as by the tongue." As James says, "See how a tiny spark sets a huge forest ablaze! The tongue is such a flame. . . . Its flames encircle our course from birth, and its fire is kindled by hell."

But how do we tame the tongue? As James says, "Every form of life, four-footed or winged, crawling or swimming, can be tamed and has been tamed by mankind; the tongue no man can tame." Try as we might, we still engage in idle talk that degenerates into gossip and slander. Try as we might, we still fall into coarse language that leads to pretensions and abusive swearing. Try as we might, we do not obey Jesus very well.

Paul gives us a hint of the answer. He says, "All of that is out of place. Instead, give thanks. . . . Be filled with the Spirit, addressing one another in psalms and hymns and inspired songs." Give thanks!! Instead of getting into negative dialogue, keep your words uplifted by positive praise and thanks for every person, place, and situation you encounter. Nobody, especially a brother or sister in Jesus, is so bad that no good can be found in him or her. Paul goes on, "Give thanks to God the Father always and for everything in the name of our Lord Jesus Christ." We can do this even for what we think is bad, because "all things work for good for those who are called."

Do we keep our words truthful? Do we keep our words positive? The gospel calls us to both. Both demand a response that is a choice. Choose to change. "Speak the truth in love." Then we will rediscover the awesome power and dignity of the spoken word. ☐

Turn the Other Cheek
Matthew 5:38-42 (11:Monday)

Offer no resistance to injury. (v. 39)

How contrary are Jesus' words and personal example to even the religious standard of this world! The law of the Jews said, "An eye for an eye, and a tooth for a tooth." Ghandi spoke of passive resistance. Granted, both Ghandi and the Jews spoke of a very high way, much superior to the greed and violence that often run rampant through the secular world. Yet neither reached the height of Jesus' teaching. Jesus' teaching on nonresistance is the highest way. There is no other way that is so pure.

Granted, the New Testament speaks of the just civil government using force to resist the unjust and the criminal. Paul says, "It is not without purpose that the ruler carries the sword; he is God's servant, to inflict his avenging wrath upon the wrong-doer. . . . Rulers cause no fear when a man does what is right, but only when his conduct is evil." John the Baptist only said to the soldiers, "Don't bully anyone. Denounce no one falsely. Be content with your wages." He didn't tell them to refrain from using the sword to establish and maintain justice.

This led to what is called the "just war theory." It was first put forward by St. Augustine, who adapted it from the writings of Cicero, the pagan philosopher. In essence, the theory says that war and force are permissible for the just Christian government only in self-defense, and then only as a last resort when the actual boundaries of a nation or state are attacked. A police force may also use force, but only under extreme circumstances. The individuals of the state are called to live the pure nonresistant standard taught by Jesus, thus substantially ruling out the use of force in private self-defense. Thus individuals are not to actually take up the sword; only the civil state takes up the sword in accord with Scripture. Pretty stringent and idealistic standards! Unfortunately, they have seldom, if ever, really been lived out, even in the heyday of European Christendom.

Jesus did say to Peter, who was defending the best person and kingdom ever to be manifested upon the earth, "Put back your sword where it belongs. Those who use the sword are sooner or later destroyed by it." Then he reached to heal his assailant's ear! Some say that the fact that the apostles had a small sword at all was only to fulfill the Scripture, "He was counted among the wicked." As St. James says in support of this nonresistance even in the face of injustice, "You condemned, even killed, the just man; he does not resist you."

This pure gospel ethic has led many in the historical church to a stance of total nonresistance. The early Christians, for the most part, held such a view. So too did many of the monastic communities. The Franciscans, both vowed brothers and sisters and lay people, were forbidden to take up arms for any reason whatsoever. Of course, the peaceful witness of the Mennonites, the Amish, and the Quakers stand out especially in later Christian tradition.

Today we all face the question of trying to stop force with force in the terrible light of the nuclear era. It is as if ultimate conclusions have been stretched to their limit. The middle ground of the idealistic "just war" may have become irrelevant. Resistance might only mean mutual widespread destruction which destroys thousands upon thousands of innocent civilian lives. Today, more than ever before in history, Jesus' teaching on nonresistance seems to me to be the only morally acceptable way.

What about us? Do we seek to justify our forceful and even violent resistance to that which we judge as our enemy? Or do we follow the example of Jesus' nonresistance in our personal life? Even the just war theory requires this passive attitude of the private Christian. Jesus was silent before his accusers. He was led like a lamb to slaughter. If we do not operate with the same gentle attitude, no political measures to stop nuclear war will succeed. We must calm the anger that explodes within our own heart before we can effectively defuse the potential of nuclear war. □

Love Unto Death!
Matthew 5:43-48 (11:Tuesday)

My command to you is: love your enemies, pray for your persecutors. This will prove that you are sons of your heavenly Father. (v. 44-45)

Here Jesus brings us to a love that is clearly beyond the realm of the natural—it is supernatural! It builds upon the spirituality of the Old Testament, but it goes far beyond. This teaching is something higher; it is something new.

Ironically, Jesus appeals to a law of nature to prove this higher way. He says of the love of the Father, "His sun rises on the bad and the good, he rains on the just and the unjust." What he cannot find among the pagans he finds in the basic law of nature. As St. Paul says, "Invisible realities, God's eternal power and divinity, have become visible, recognized through the things he has made." If we would really open our eyes to the natural we could learn of the supernatural. As it is, most of the natural world is blinded to itself, so it cannot find God.

I am not talking about self-centeredness or even about loving only when it is easy, when it is not a sacrifice. Jesus says, "If you love those who love you, what merit is there in that? Do not tax collectors do as much? And if you greet your brothers only, what is so praiseworthy about that? Do not pagans do as much?"

Most of us want to love as much as we can. It makes life more pleasant for us; it makes us more popular. As Sirach says, "Say nothing harmful, small or great; be not a foe instead of a friend; a bad name and disgrace will you acquire." A love of this sort just makes good common sense. It's even good for business! To help the poor or the hurting is actually good for yourself, as long as helping them does not bring you unnecessary pain, poverty, or inconvenience. The problem is that it is really nothing more than love of self.

This is where the world's love stops and Jesus' kind of love keeps on going. Jesus actually became poor himself to help the poor. He actually died to help the dying! This is why his kind of love is called sacrificial. It gives up itself to save another.

Yet it is precisely because of this humble "love unto death" that Jesus experienced resurrection glory. Paul says, "And it was thus that he humbled himself, obediently accepting even death, death on a cross! Because of this, God highly exalted him."

If we totally die to self, we can break through to a new life. If we die to our present understanding of the natural, we break through to the supernatural. This brings us to a new joy! As St. Peter says, "If you should have to suffer for justice' sake, happy will you be. . . . Rejoice instead, in the measure you share Christ's sufferings. When his glory is revealed, you will rejoice exultantly."

Do we give and sacrifice with this kind of joy? Is our love self-centered, or is it truly centered on God and neighbor? Has our selfishness so blinded us that we can no longer even read the universal law of nature which teaches us of the supernatural? Take a chance and love foolishly—even when it costs you to do it. Then you will break through to a whole new life filled with unspeakable joy! Then the blinders will fall from your eyes, and all the world will become exciting and new! □

The Right Humility
Matthew 6:1-6,16-18 (11:Wednesday)

Keep your deeds of mercy secret, and your Father who sees in secret will repay you. (v. 4)

Last week we heard Jesus say, "Your light must shine before men so that they may see the goodness of your acts." Today he says, "Keep your deeds of mercy secret." Is this a contradiction? The answer is no. Together these words form a whole. One cannot be fully understood without the other.

Jesus was well aware of the people of his own day who lived a religion for show. He says of the scribes and Pharisees, "Their words are bold but their deeds are few. . . . All their works are performed to be seen." They "like to parade around in their robes and accept marks of respect in public, front seats in the synagogues, and places of honor at banquets. These men devour the savings of widows and recite long prayers for appearance' sake." Needless to say, Jesus had strong feelings about this kind of religion. He said to those who practiced it, "Woe to you, scribes and Pharisees, you frauds!"

Paul also encountered such religion. He says of some, "They make a pretense of religion but negate its power. Stay clear of them." He fought against a tendency to return to external Jewish observances in Galatia when he wrote, "How can you return to those powerless, worthless, natural elements to which you seem willing to enslave yourselves once more? You even go so far as to keep the ceremonial observance of days and months, seasons and years! I fear for you; all my efforts with you may have been wasted." Paul was frightened that such practices would lead them back to the very pride and self-righteous religion Jesus so strongly condemned. "While these make a certain show of wisdom in their affected piety, humility, and bodily austerity, their chief effect is that they indulge men's pride."

Jesus strikes the balance in his teaching on the Lord's Prayer. He says, "In your prayer do not rattle on like the pagans." Then he proceeds to teach us a prayer. It is simple, short, and humble. Yet it includes all the basic aspects of a personal love relationship with God, which is the goal of all prayer.

The same thing is true of Jesus' teaching on fasting. He condemns those who fast "so that others may see they are fasting." Then he goes on to teach us to fast. He says, "When you fast . . ." He does not say we shouldn't fast!

We should let our Christian works shine like lights to the world, yet we should never perform our works just to be seen. We should be "children of God beyond reproach in the midst of a twisted and depraved generation—among whom you shine like stars in the sky." Yet, "your life is hidden now with Christ in God." There must be balance here. This balance brings humility. It keeps our prayers and actions sincere.

Are we sincere? Or do we pray in order to impress, and humbly work in order to look "spiritual"?   □

Private Prayer
Matthew 6:7-15 (11:Thursday)

This is how you are to pray. (v. 9)

As we saw yesterday, Jesus was ardently opposed to a religion for show. His teaching on prayer is no exception. Jesus says, "When you are praying, do not behave like the hypocrites who love to stand and pray in synagogues or on street corners in order to be noticed.... Whenever you pray, go to your room, close your door, and pray to your Father in private. Then your Father, who sees what no man sees, will repay you." As St. Paul says, "Your life is hidden now with Christ in God. When Christ our life appears, then you shall appear with him in glory."

Jesus was a man of solitude. He went to the desert before he began his public ministry. Even during his ministry he was constantly retiring from the crowds to pray in seclusion. In Luke's Gospel he withdrew before his Sermon on the Mount. Likewise, he sought refuge in solitude before he chose the twelve, the "community" with which he was to minister and found his church! He was in prayerful solitude when he was transfigured in the mystical light of Mount Tabor. And he was in solitude before he met the final challenge of his ministry, the cross. As St. Luke's Gospel says, "He often retired to deserted places and prayed."

St. Paul also spent time in solitude and silence: "The gospel I proclaimed to you is no mere human invention. I did not receive it from any man, nor was I schooled in it. It came by revelation from Jesus Christ.... Without seeking human advisors, or even going to Jerusalem to see those who were apostles before me, I went off to Arabia; later I returned to Damascus. Three years after that I went up to Jerusalem to get to know Cephas.... Then, after fourteen years, I went up to Jerusalem again." Paul does not say how long he was in solitude. He probably stayed in the desert at least forty days, after the example of Jesus and the Old Testament saints.

Mind you, this is the same Paul who encouraged the charismatics at Corinth to "set your hearts on spiritual gifts—above all the gifts of prophecy ... and do not forbid those who speak in tongues." But he warned the prophets and tongue speakers,

"Since you have set your hearts on spiritual gifts, try to be rich in those that build up the church." Against the charismatic confusion that often results when everyone wants to utter a prayer or prophecy, "You may all speak your prophecies, but one by one, so that all may be instructed and encouraged. . . . Make sure that everything is done properly and in order."

We are reminded of St. Francis's words to preachers: "Their words should be examined and chaste." Also, Proverbs reminds us that we should never be "hasty in our words" but should think hard before we speak.

Are we more willing to speak than to listen? If we listen to God's abundant words to us in prayer, then our words to each other will be few but spiritually abundant. Do we try to impress others with our prayers, or do we pray only to please God and edify the church? It is easy to impress; edification is more difficult. □

Resist the Darkness
Matthew 6:19-23 (11:Friday)

Remember, where your treasure is, there your heart is also. (v. 21)

This is perhaps the highest reason and motivation to embrace what we call "gospel poverty." Because of our sin it is very difficult to use God's material blessings without making a false god out of them. Instead of the beauty and abundant goodness of creation leading us to praise the Creator, our sin causes us to worship the creature. Instead of using our possessions, they begin to possess us. This is nothing short of idolatry on our part, and possession on the part of the spirits of this world!

As the Book of Wisdom says of God's goodness coming to us in creation, "All good things together came to me in her company. . . . I rejoiced in them all, because Wisdom is their leader. . . . Yet all men were by nature foolish who from the good things seen did not succeed in knowing him who is, and from studying the works did not discern the artisan. . . . Now if out of joy in their beauty they thought them gods, let them know how far more excellent is the Lord than these; for the original source of beauty fashioned them. . . . For from the greatness and the beauty of created things their original author, by analogy, is seen."

As St. Paul says to the Romans, "Since the creation of the world, invisible realities, God's eternal power and divinity, have become visible, recognized through the things he has made. Therefore, these men are inexcusable. . . . They exchanged the glory of the immortal God for images. . . . They did not see fit to acknowledge God, so God delivered them up to their own depraved sense to do what is unseemly." Paul also says that it is actually demonic spirits influencing such carnally oriented people: "You gave allegiance to the present age and to the prince of the air, the spirit who is even now at work in the rebellious."

In today's gospel Jesus speaks of materialism as a source of spiritual darkness in our life: "The eye is the body's lamp. If your eyes are good, your body will be filled with light; if your eyes are bad, your body will be in darkness. And if your light is darkness, how deep will the darkness be!" To be materialistic is to be idolatrous! To be materialistic is to be at least influenced, if not possessed, by the spirit of the world through our own possessions. It brings darkness!

Today Jesus warns us that our possessions actually possess us. If we have more than we really need, we increase the risk of losing our soul. God wants us to enjoy his goodness through creation, but he does not want us to be materialistic. Use what you need joyfully, but freely satisfying all your wants will surely lead you to the spiritual darkness that comes from hell. Discern between wants and needs. God wants to meet our needs, but the unchecked satisfaction of all our wants will never satisfy our most basic need—healthy spiritual life!

Do we have more than we really need? Does the pursuit of our wants take up our precious energy, time, and money? These commodities could be better used in serving God. They could better glorify God by being used for the benefit of the poor.

Are we possessed by possessions? Do we worship the creation more than we worship the Creator? If we worship the Creator, we will use the creation only according to his plan. If we set our heart on God, we will have little taste for wealth. Yet if we direct our energy toward wealth, our heart will have little time for God. □

The Freedom of Poverty
Matthew 6:24-34 (11:Saturday)

You cannot give yourself to God and money. I warn you, then: do not worry about your livelihood, what you are to eat or drink or use for clothing. . . . Seek first his kingship over you, his way of holiness, and all these things will be given you besides. (v. 24-25, 33)

The final reason for voluntary gospel poverty is the attainment of freedom. The more you have, the more you have to be concerned with; the more time and energy you spend on things, the less you have for the things of the kingdom.

As to the material responsibilities that go with getting married and raising a family, Paul says, "The unmarried man is busy with the Lord's affairs, concerned with pleasing the Lord; but the married man is busy with the world's demands and occupied with pleasing his wife. . . . I am going into this with you for your own good. I have no desire to place restrictions on you, but I do want to promote what is good, what will help you to devote yourselves entirely to the Lord." For Paul, marriage meant more material concerns, and more material concerns meant time and energy taken away from the Lord. This is why so many who are celibate for Jesus have also embraced the poverty of Jesus. The two go hand in hand.

But Jesus' teaching is not just a matter for celibates; it is a matter for all who follow Christ. Jesus says, "None of you can be my disciple if he does not renounce all his possessions." St. Paul says of this universal renunciation, "From now on those with wives should live as though they had none, . . . buyers should conduct themselves as though they owned nothing, and those who make use of the world as though they were not using it." Jesus says, "Consider the lilies."

Imagine a flower. It can grow in its natural environment in a grassy field, high on a mountain, in a meadow, or in a deep wilderness wood. Yet it can also grow in a city building's windowbox or rooftop garden. It can even grow up through the cracks in the pavement, for that matter!

We might find ourself in a community of celibate monks in a mountain hermitage or raising an inner city family of ten or twelve children. No matter. We are called to total gospel poverty either way. We deny ourselves everything so that others might benefit from God in everything. Thus we gain a hundredfold blessing in everything. Internally both ways of life are the same; they just have a different external expression.

Are we really free of the possessions we use? Do we use them, or do they abuse us? Are we free, or are we slaves? If we find ourselves enslaved, it is time to simplify. Better yet, if we find ourselves slaves to material things, it is time to totally renounce our own desire for them so that we will use them only out of love for others. If we are to be slaves, it is better to be a slave of love. Then we will be truly free.   □

The Proper Judgment
Matthew 7:1-5 (12:Monday)

If you want to avoid judgment, stop passing judgment. . . . Remove the plank from your own eye first; then you will see clearly to take the speck from your brother's eye. (v. 1, 5)

The Scripture is full of admonitions on why we shouldn't judge. Perhaps it is because judgment is such a horrible problem among us mortals. We are always trying to be God!

James says, "Do not, my brothers, speak ill of one another. The one who speaks ill of his brother or judges his brother is speaking against the law. It is the law he judges. If, however, you judge the law you are no observer of the law, you are its judge. There is but one Lawgiver and Judge, one who can save and destroy. Who then are you to judge your neighbor?"

Paul brings out other aspects of this question of judgment: "It matters little to me whether you or any human court pass judgment on me. I do not even pass judgment on myself. . . . The Lord is the one to judge one, so stop passing judgment before the time of his return." Paul says he does not even judge himself! He just does his best and keeps moving forward. Likewise, he is not ashamed of reminding others to "get off his case."

This does not mean there is absolutely no proper judgment in the church. Jesus clearly gave the power of the keys to Peter and the apostles: "If you forgive men's sins, they are forgiven them; if you hold them bound, they are held bound.... I will entrust to you the keys of the kingdom of God." Concerning the problem of the sexually immoral brother in Corinth Paul said, "What business is it of mine to judge outsiders? Is it not those inside the community you must judge? God will judge the others. 'Expel the wicked man from your midst.'" Concerning the scandal of taking inner-church problems to the secular courts he said, "How can anyone with a case against another dare bring it for judgment to the wicked and not to God's holy people? Do you not know that the believers will judge the world? If the judgment of the world is to be yours, are you to be thought unworthy of judging in minor matters? Do you not know that we are to judge the angels? Surely, then, we are up to deciding everyday affairs. If you have such matters to decide, do you accept as judges those who have no standing in the church? I say this in an attempt to shame you. Can it be there is no one among you wise enough to settle a case between one member of the church and another?" Paul clearly recognized the power of the leader of the church to judge matters of correct faith and morality within the community.

Furthermore, today's gospel does call us to a healthy examination of ourselves: "Remove the plank from your own eye first." This implies a healthy self-judgment—not a self-judgment that cripples but one that brings life and positive growth.

Today we seem so unwilling to submit to scriptural teachings. We do not want to stop judging one another, yet we do not want to submit to the judgment of the church either. Furthermore, we do not want to judge ourselves;—we want to do exactly what we want. No limits! We all want to be God. We all want to be the pope. We all want to be bishops. We don't say that, but we say it by our unwillingness to submit to their judgment. So we continue to judge others and let ourselves slide and so propagate more disobedience, the root of all sin. Therefore our judgment is futile, for it only propagates sin, and all sin must be judged. It is a vicious cycle from which no human can break free. We make bad gods. True, most of us would make bad popes and bishops.

Let us begin judging ourselves and stop judging others. Let us begin to grow and to allow others to grow. Let us be obedient to God and those within the church to whom Jesus himself has given the power to judge. Then truth and love will finally triumph over unrighteous judgment and sin. □

The Gospel without Compromise
Matthew 7:6, 12-14 (12:Tuesday)

Do not give what is holy to dogs or toss your pearls before swine. . . . Enter through the narrow gate. (v. 6, 13)

Do we compromise our call to live the gospel in order to simply reach more people? Do we water down its salty taste so that more people can swallow it? Jesus says today, "How narrow is the gate that leads to life, how rough the road, and how few there are who find it!" Jesus assures us that the gospel will not be received by the masses, therefore we should not compromise it in order to reach larger groups of people. He says, "Many are called, but few are chosen." Jesus is interested in quality, not quantity!

Yet there is a certain amount of moderation involved in giving witness to the world. Jesus does say, "You are to be my witnesses . . . even to the ends of the earth." Paul says, "Work with your hands as we directed you to do, so that you will give good example to outsiders and want for nothing. . . . Avoid any semblance of evil." Peter is also conscious of this witness when he says, "Who indeed can harm you if you are committed deeply to doing what is right? . . . Should anyone ask you the reason for this hope of yours, be ever ready to reply, but speak gently and respectfully." No doubt, the problems the early Christians had with civil governments also led the apostles to their admonitions about obeying the government. It cannot be denied: The apostles were definitely sensitive to the world's response to their message and life-style.

There is also a healthy discretion and moderation encouraged within the Christian community! "We who are strong in faith should be patient with the scruples of those whose faith is weak; we must not be selfish." In matters of little importance we are to defer to our neighbor.

Concerning devotional practices Paul says, "The kingdom of God is not a matter of eating and drinking, but of justice, peace, and the joy that is given by the Holy Spirit." Yet he concedes,

"Extend a kind welcome to those who are weak in faith. Do not enter into disputes with them. A man of sound faith knows he can eat anything, while one who is weak in faith eats only vegetables." To the Corinthians he says, "Food does not bring us closer to God. We suffer no loss through failing to eat, and we gain no favor by eating. Take care, however, lest in exercising your right you become an occasion of sin to the weak." In other words, if it really isn't that important anyway, compromise for the sake of your weaker brother or sister.

Paul himself took a Nazarite vow in order to prove his sincerity to those under the law and to bring them into the freedom of the new law! This vow did not go against his conscience, for its small demands did not conflict with the greater demands of the gospel. As Paul says, "I made myself a slave of all so as to win over as many as possible.... I have made myself all things to all men in order to save at least some of them."

Yet we are not to compromise the essence of the gospel. John says, "Have no love for the world, nor the things that the world affords.... Carnal allurements, enticements for the eye, the life of empty show.... The world with its seductions is passing away, but the man who does God's will endures forever."

Do we compromise or defer? A compromise is for ourselves, and it touches an essential of the faith. A deferment is for the sake of others, and it concerns mere externals. Too many small deferments can easily build into a compromise. Has our life as individuals and as a church been slowly compromised?

Is there really any visible difference between us and the world? There should be. If there is not, then we have gone too far. As John says, "Keep oneself unspotted from the world." Do not compromise with the world in order to save it, for then you and the world will both be lost. □

Guarding against Wolves
Matthew 7:15-20 (12:Wednesday)

Be on your guard against false prophets, who come to you in sheep's clothing but underneath are wolves on the prowl. (v. 15)

We must not become paranoid about evil in the church, but we should not be naive either. Jesus promised that Satan would deceive many by taking on the appearance of a prophet of God. People aren't completely stupid; they have been created in the very image of God! They do not usually follow something that is obviously evil or wrong, but they will follow evil if it appears to be good. They will be, and have been since the beginning of time, all too ready to believe a half-truth. This is Satan's most popular tool.

Such also was the experience within the early church. Paul says, "Satan disguises himself as an angel of light. It comes as no surprise that his ministers disguise themselves as ministers of the justice of God." He writes to his spiritual son Timothy, "In later times some will turn away from the faith and will heed deceitful spirits and things taught by demons through plausible liars. . . . They make a pretense of religion but negate its power, . . . always learning but never able to reach a knowledge of the truth. . . . With perverted minds they falsify the faith."

Sound familiar? Isn't this the sentiment of many in today's church? Perhaps these words will give us hope and courage when we hear the theologians of our own time entering into intellectual speculations that only mold God's truth to the image of our sin, rather than allowing God's power in Jesus to mold us to the image of God.

The final test of theology is spiritual fruit. Today's gospel says, "You can tell a tree by its fruit." Paul says, "False doctrines . . . promote idle speculations rather than that training in faith which God requires. What we are aiming at in this warning is the love that springs from a pure heart, a good conscience, and sincere faith. Have nothing to do with senseless, ignorant disputations. As you well know, they only breed quarrels." To the church in Corinth he says, "My fear is that, just as the serpent seduced Eve by his cunning, your thoughts may be corrupted, and you may fall away from your sincere and complete devotion to Christ."

Of course, the "good fruit" of the true faith can only be brought forth in the Spirit. Paul says, "The fruit of the Spirit is love, joy, peace, patient endurance, kindness, generosity, faith, mildness, and chastity." He also lists the contrary: "It is obvious what proceeds from the flesh: lewd conduct, impurity, licentiousness, idolatry, sorcery, hostilities, bickering, jealousy, outbursts of rage, selfish rivalries, dissensions, factions, envy, drunkenness, orgies and the like." Right belief brings forth right practice. You cannot have right practice in God's eyes if you do not first have right faith.

Many of those in today's church who are trying to justify such sins through theological speculation are doing so because they have yet to experience the full power of the Holy Spirit in their lives. Yes, they believe! "Even the demons believe and tremble," says James. But they do not fully submit to the power of the Spirit, so they remain powerless in overcoming their own personal sin, much less that of those they pastor and counsel.

What about us? It's easy to sit in judgment of theologians. But issues of faith and sexual morality are not the only things on the list. Paul puts bickering, jealousy, outbursts of rage, and so on right up there with the "biggies." We might have right belief without right practice in these areas. It is not enough to be orthodox, we must be holy. Yet we cannot be fully holy without orthodoxy.

What about us? Do we try to justify our personal sin? If we do we are no better than those who openly propagate theological error. ☐

Do You Know Jesus?
Matthew 7:21-29 (12:Thursday)

None of those who cry out, "Lord, Lord," will enter the kingdom of God, but only the one who does the will of my Father in heaven. (v. 21)

It is not enough to be religious or even Christian to enter the kingdom. St. Augustine says that baptism will leave an indelible mark upon the souls of many who go to hell! It is not enough to be a baptized Christian. We must actually live the Christian life.

Nor is it enough to be charismatic or born again. These are all external classifications for interior religious movements. The kingdom is primarily internal. Many of the things done by those rejected by Jesus closely resemble the earmarks of those involved in seemingly Spirit-led renewal. "Have we not exorcised demons by its power? Did we not do many miracles in your name as well?"

These are all great gifts of the Spirit if they are genuine. Paul says, "There are different gifts but the same Spirit. . . . To one the Spirit gives wisdom in discourse, to another the power to express knowledge. Through the Spirit one receives faith, . . . another is given the gift of healing, . . . and still another miraculous powers. Prophecy is given to one; to another power to distinguish one spirit from another. One receives the gift of tongues, another that of interpreting the tongues."

But these manifestations are not always a sure test of the authenticity of the presence of the Holy Spirit. John says, "Beloved, do not trust every spirit, but put the spirits to a test to see if they belong to God, because many false prophets have appeared in the world." Paul says, "Satan disguises himself as an angel of light." Many heresies in Christian history have had all of the earmarks of being fully charismatic, empowered by a Pente-costal outpouring of the Holy Spirit. But their propagators did not really know the Spirit of Jesus. This is the key, in my opinion. Jesus says to those seemingly Spirit-filled people, "I never knew you. Out of my sight, you evildoers!"

Do we know Jesus? Adam "knew" Eve through intercourse, where "the two became one." Have we actually become one with Jesus? John says, "The man who claims to abide in him conducts himself just as he did." If we have become one with him, we will do the works of Jesus, for he will be working through us. John says, "No one begotten of God acts sinfully because he remains of God's stock; he cannot sin because he is begotten of God." We cannot perform works that claim to be charismatic, but destroy personal lives and split the churches. We must take the words of Jesus and put them into practice, or perhaps we do not really know him yet.   □

The Old and the New
Matthew 8:1-4 (12:Friday)

I do will it. Be cured. . . . Go and show yourself to the priest and offer the gift Moses prescribed. That should be the proof they need. (v. 3, 4)

Jesus cured. But he also worked through and with the recognized religious authority of his day. Did he have to work in union with the Mosaic law? Probably not. He was, after all, God incarnate come to establish a whole new religious order by giving us the new covenant. The Old Testament was passing away. Yet Jesus still worked through the vessel of the old while establishing the new, both for the sake of the people still under the old and for the sake of God the Father, who established the old as well as the new.

Of the old he says, "Do not think I have come to abolish the law and the prophets. I have come, not to abolish them, but to fulfill them." Regarding the authority of the religious leaders of the day he says, "The scribes and the Pharisees have succeeded Moses as teachers; therefore, do everything and observe everything they tell you. But do not follow their example. . . . Unless your holiness surpasses that of the scribes and Pharisees you shall not enter the kingdom of God."

Even Paul, who so adamantly resisted a return to the Judaic law, says, "Yet the law is holy and the commandment is holy and just and good. . . . It was only through the law that I came to know sin." But he goes on, "Now we have been released from the law—for we have died to what bound us—and we serve in the new spirit, not the antiquated letter." And, "He who loves his neighbor has fulfilled the law." And again, "The fruit of the Spirit is love, joy, peace. . . . Against such there is no law."

In other words, we more than fulfill the law when the Spirit inspires us with a new love for God and people. But we do so out of love, not out of legalism and fear. The law only sets a minimum requirement for holiness. We surpass the law. We really do not need it anymore; yet we do not deny it, we fulfill it.

In many ways the same holds true for church law. It sets minimum guidelines of holiness for following Jesus by giving us doctrines, devotions, and sacraments. Likewise, it points out the grave moral disorder of our time which we call sin. But a mere observance of the law will not guarantee a living relationship with Jesus Christ. We must fulfill the law out of love. We far surpass its minimal requirements when we are empowered with the Spirit.

In fulfilling the law we also "show ourselves to the priest." We still work within the church. If we are healed by the Spirit, we still seek the sacrament of the anointing of the sick so that the healing might be confirmed and strengthened by the God-given authority of the church. Likewise, if we experience the overwhelming wonder of God's forgiveness through prayer, we confirm and strengthen that experience through the sacrament of reconciliation. I say "strengthen" because the authority God has in fact given the corporate body of the church in such matters cannot but bolster a spiritual reality we already begin to experience privately.

Do we submit to the church in such matters? Do we recognize the goodness of the law, as well as its limitations? We must know the balance between the two before we fully experience God's truth.   □

Take a New Look
Matthew 8:5-17 (12:Saturday)

I assure you, I have never found this much faith in Israel. (v. 10)

Sometimes it is those outside our religious structures who really have faith in God. Those of us within the structures have been given the Scriptures, the doctrines, and the sacraments. We enjoy God's benefits constantly. But we must get beyond the external aids God has given us. We must really find God. Sometimes it takes the genuine faith of one outside the church to remind us of this.

Paul speaks similarly concerning the old covenant: "It is not those who hear the law who are just in the sight of God; it is those who keep it who will be declared just. When Gentiles who do not have the law keep it as by instinct, these men although without the law serve as a law for themselves. They show that the demands of the law are written in their hearts. Their conscience bears witness together with that law."

This is not to say that Paul didn't think that the Jews benefited greatly by their covenant with God. "What advantage, then, of being a Jew, and what value is there in circumcision? The answer is, much in every respect. First of all, the Jews were entrusted with the words of God." And later Paul said, "Theirs were the adoption, the covenants, the law-giving, the worship, and the promise." Jesus also recognized the authority of the Jewish leaders: "The scribes and the Pharisees have succeeded Moses as teachers; therefore, do and observe everything they tell you."

The same holds true for the new covenant in the church. Our bishops are successors to the apostles. Our pope succeeds St. Peter, whom Jesus ordained leader of the Twelve in his absence. Through them we have the Scriptures, the sacraments, doctrines established with apostolic authority, and the example of radical Christian living. We have been richly blessed by God.

Yet it is often those outside the church or newcomers to the church who appreciate these gifts most. Those who live with these rich blessings every day tend to take them for granted.

Do we take our faith for granted? Do we appreciate the blessings of the church as much as those who see them with new eyes? Furthermore, do we, with all our God-given aids and graces, really have as much faith in God as many of those who do not call themselves Catholic or even Christian? □

Help for the Homeless
Matthew 8:18-22 (13:Monday)

The foxes have lairs, the birds in the sky have nests, but the Son of Man has nowhere to lay his head. (v. 20)

Jesus was an itinerant. He was a penniless wanderer who forsook the right to personal property in order to bring others into the wealth of the kingdom of God. In this sense, Jesus actually does not offer a practical alternative life-style for the average disciple.

The Scriptures speak of three major gospel approaches to wealth and poverty. The first is the literal example of Jesus in Matthew 10: "Provide yourselves with neither gold nor silver nor copper in your belts!" The second is found in Acts 2: "Those who believed shared all things in common." The third is found in St. Paul's letters to the church in Corinth: "Those with wives should live as though they had none, . . . buyers should conduct themselves as though they owned nothing, and those who make use of the world as though they were not using it. . . . The relief of others ought not to impoverish you; there should be a certain equality."

Of the classical expressions of Christianity, the first approach is represented by the mendicant orders (the Franciscans, Dominicans, Carmelites, and others), the second by monks, and the third by the average Christian. Far from relegating the laity to a third-rate Christianity, this challenges all Christians to live the gospel more radically according to their proper state of life. How many Franciscans (including this writer) actually live according to the absolute poverty of Matthew 10? How many monks have totally renounced personal ownership in favor of the equal common life of Acts 2? How many lay people, married or single, really use the things of this world in the detachment and poverty of spirit that brings an eventual equality between the rich and the poor?

Unfortunately, some families are forced to live according to the patterns of the itinerant mendicants. Many families in this world actually have no homes. Due to social injustice, many live as refugees and outcasts, forced to flee for their lives from one country to the next. Many who do have homes live in a state of destitution and poverty we would never deem socially acceptable, even for the poor of our own country. Truly, they live as pilgrims and strangers, not by choice but because of oppression, injustice, and uncaring greed.

Do we help the refugees of our world? What about illegal aliens who flee an injustice in their own land? Do we help them by simply turning them away? No, we do not. Ironically, turning them away does not help us either. As Paul says, "Your plenty at the present time should supply their need so that their surplus may one day supply your need, with equality as the result."

We must be willing to truly embrace the "equality" spoken of by St. Paul in order to help the poor of this world. We must take appropriate private and corporate church and civil action in order to stop the injustice and help our brothers and sisters in need. In the long run we will not only save their lives, but we will save ourselves. □

Expect and Accept
Matthew 8:23-27 (13:Tuesday)

"Lord, save us! We are lost!" . . . *"Where is your courage? How little faith you have!"* (v. 25, 26)

It is easy being a Christian when all goes well, but how about when the going gets tough? It's easy to go with Jesus in the boat when there is smooth sailing, but it is more difficult when the waters are rough. How true is the statement, "When the going gets tough, the tough get going."

Jesus does call us to a fully expectant faith. This is different from a faith that simply accepts—this is a faith that expects! Jesus says, "If you are ready to believe that you will receive whatever you ask for in prayer, it shall be done for you." This kind of faith requires great expectation. Jesus says, "I solemnly assure you, whoever says to this mountain, 'Be lifted up and thrown into the sea,' and has no inner doubts, but believes that what he says will happen, shall have it done for him." Don't just accept—expect! But you must be willing to accept, or your expectation becomes presumption.

This process involves a lot of positive visualization. The mind thinks in images. In order to believe in something before we ask in prayer, it is helpful to visualize it. As Jesus says, "The mouth speaks whatever fills the mind." In a sense you could say we "visualize" something into existence before we ask for it in prayer.

God is very concerned about our thought process. Scripture says, "Whatever you think you will become." It also speaks of the "spiritual renewal of the mind." It is said, "He keeps him in perfect peace whose mind is stayed on thee."

But what happens when we step out in faith and our peace doesn't come? Peter stepped out into the water and began to sink. In today's gospel the disciples went with Jesus in the boat, but the storm waves rose up anyway! We must not only expect, we must accept. Otherwise expectation is not really faith—it is presumption.

St. Paul says, "We know that God makes all things work together for the good." It takes great faith to believe that even the storm waves work for good. We look into the world and see great trouble and tragedy. We see suffering and pain, hunger, war, and the ever-present threat of technological holocaust. It is hard to thank God for such things! It is hard to have such accepting faith! As Jesus says about the time toward the end, "You will hear of wars and rumors of wars. . . . Nation will rise against nation, and one kingdom against another. There will be famine and pestilence and earthquakes." He even speaks of grave personal harm: "They will hand you over to torture and kill you. Indeed, you will be hated by all nations on my account. . . . Because of the increase of evil, the love of most will grow cold." In the midst of all this he says, "Do not be alarmed."

How can we not be alarmed without a faith that believes that "all things work together for the good" in God's plan? It is such faith that allowed St. Paul to "thank God always and for everything." It is this trust that allowed Jesus to be "sleeping soundly" in the midst of the storm. It was the disciples' lack of such faith that caused them to cry out, "We are lost!"

How do we respond to the storms in our life? Do we join with Jesus in sleeping peacefully in the boat, knowing that even in our trials and distress our "heavenly Father cares for us"? Or do we cry out in fear and alarm to God to "save us"? It wasn't wrong for the disciples to ask for help; but their alarm, their lack of faith, was what was wrong. Let us ask for a miracle in expectant faith, but let us peacefully accept the crosses that come our way. The crosses are given to us as a grace that brings us to resurrection!

Today let us face the storms of our life with true and calm faith.   □

God versus Mammon
Matthew 8:28-34 (13:Wednesday)

The entire town came out to meet Jesus. When they caught sight of him, they begged him to leave their neighborhood. (v. 34)

Jesus Christ is not always good for business. If we let Jesus cast all the demons out of our life, we may even have to change our way of earning a living. If Jesus changes our personal morality, then he will also affect our business.

Jesus says, "You cannot give yourself to God and money. I warn you, then: do not worry about your livelihood. . . . Seek first his kingship over you, his way of holiness, and all these things will be given you besides."

St. Paul also strikes a practical yet uncompromising balance: "Buyers should conduct themselves as though they owned nothing, and those who make use of the world as though they were not using it, for the world as we know is passing away. I should like you to be free of all worries."

Revelation also speaks about business. It warns against a Christianity that compromises with blatant commercialism: "Fallen, fallen is Babylon the great! She has become a dwelling place for demons. . . . The kings of the earth committed fornication with her, and the world's merchants grew rich from her wealth and wantonness."

Christianity cannot be compromised by commercialism. The "almighty dollar" must never replace the one true God. Yes, we must live in the world, but we must never be of the world. Jesus prayed to his Father, "I do not ask you to take them out of the world, but to guard them from the evil one. They are not of the world, any more than I belong to the world." And St. John says, "Have no love for the world, nor the things that the world affords. If anyone loves the world, the Father's love has no place in him, for nothing that the world affords comes from the Father." St. Paul similarly says, "The flesh in its tendency is at enmity with God."

It is not only the spiritual dimension of detachment from possessions that makes Jesus so much a threat to our materialistic and commercial world. It is also his practical teaching about sharing our wealth with the poor, words that threaten the entrepreneurs of the West. Jesus says, "Sell what you have and give to the poor." The early church of Jerusalem "shared all things in common, . . . dividing everything on the basis of each one's need." Even St. Paul, in a very permissive application of Jesus' words, says, "There should be a certain equality" between the rich and the poor.

Does such equality exist between the rich and poor of Christendom? I am afraid not. Be it between individual members of our local churches or between the first and third world church, scriptural gospel equality is still a far cry from our present expression of Christianity.

Does the commercialization of Christianity really affect our daily life-style? Yes, it does! The selling of religious books, tapes, and records and the financing of large media and crusade ministries definitely affect many of our decisions that would more properly be made by spiritual standards alone. Masses of people are affected by books, records, and other ministries that gear their message to what they think will sell. Even a bishop must sometimes make decisions based on economy. Of course, God can work through such externals to manifest and accomplish his will, but according to gospel teachings, economy should not dictate spirituality. Rather, spirituality should affect economy.

Today we must make these decisions properly. We stand before two doors of human history. We must decide through which door we must pass: the door of spirituality rather than that of commercialism. If we choose wrongly, we and perhaps the entire world will perish. □

The Gifts Come from God
Matthew 9:1-8 (13:Thursday)

Why do you harbor evil thoughts? Which is less trouble to say, "Your sins are forgiven" or "Stand up and walk"? (v. 4-5)

Often in the church it would be so simple to reach out and minister God's love, yet the external religiosity and devotional scruples of others keep us from operating fully in God's power. The attitudes of misinformed laity or jealous clergy often hold us back. A person receives a healing through the prayers of a layperson, and some people immediately doubt the healing's authenticity because it didn't involve the prayers of a priest or the sacrament of the sick. Or a lay evangelist is not taken seriously only because he or she is not an ordained priest. There is nothing wrong with ordained ministries and sacraments, but God can and does work outside of these valid structures through the laity of the church.

No doubt, the apostles had to deal with such attitudes on the part of the Jews. The apostles were not educated as rabbis, yet they taught with authority. The Acts of the Apostles says of the "ordained" Sanhedrin, "Observing the self-assurance of Peter and John, and realizing that the speakers were uneducated men of no standing, the questioners were amazed."

The rabbis said the same thing about Jesus. "Where did this man get such wisdom and miraculous powers? Isn't this the carpenter's son? Isn't Mary known to be his mother and James, Joseph, Simon, and Judas his brothers? Aren't his sisters our neighbors? Where did he get all this?"

Jesus tells them where his knowledge and power came from. "My doctrine is not my own; it comes from him who sent me." To the apostles and disciples he says, "Do not worry about what you will say or how you will say it.... You will be given what you are to say. You yourselves will not be the speakers; the Spirit of your Father will be speaking in you." Even the educated St. Paul did not rely on this humanly taught wisdom when he spoke of faith in Christ: "I did not come proclaiming God's testimony with any particular eloquence or 'wisdom'. . . . My message and my preaching had none of the persuasive force of 'wise' argumentation, but the convincing power of the Spirit." As Paul says, "The gospel I proclaimed to you is no mere human invention. I did not receive it from any man, nor was I schooled in it. It came by revelation from Jesus Christ." It is the Spirit of God himself who made Jesus and the first apostles the mighty preachers they were!

The charismatic gifts of the Spirit were definitely at work among the laity as well as among the apostles. All through the Acts of the Apostles we hear of the apostles exercising leadership in light of their ordination from Jesus, but we also see prophets and evangelists of both sexes of the laity. The gifts in Corinth included "apostles, prophets, teachers, miracle workers, healers, assistants, administrators, and those who speak in tongues." While all things were to be "done properly and in order," they were not to "forbid those who speak in tongues." As Paul said to the Thessalonians, "Do not stifle the Spirit. Do not despise prophecies."

This does not mean we don't submit our charismatic gift to the church. Even Paul sought the scrutiny of the apostles, who had authority in the church, "to make sure the course I was pursuing, or had pursued, was not useless." Granted, these gifts are often raised up by the Spirit without any human intervention. But they must be submitted to the teaching authority of the church if they are to be rightly tested. As John says, "Test the spirits." And as Paul says with apostolic authority, "There are many irresponsible teachers. . . . These must be silenced."

How do we respond to the gifts of the Spirit working among the unordained of the church? Do we "harbor evil thoughts" against those we do not think qualified? God often works most mightily through the least in our midst. Let us be properly submitted to the teaching authority of the church through our ordained ministers, but let us also be open to the gifts of the Spirit working in all the people of the church.   □

Follow with Love
Matthew 9:9-13 (13:Friday)

He said to him, "Follow me." Matthew got up and followed him. Now it happened that, while Jesus was at table in Matthew's home, many tax collectors and those known as sinners came to join Jesus and his disciples at dinner. . . . "It is mercy I desire and not sacrifice." (v. 9-10, 13)

Jesus' call requires radical and immediate response. But it also requires a response that is livable. Jesus calls all his disciples to a radical response: "Follow me, and let the dead bury the dead." "If a man wishes to come after me, he must deny his very self, take up his cross, and begin to follow in my footsteps." "If you seek perfection, go, sell your possessions, and give to the poor. You will then have treasure in heaven. Afterward, come back and follow me." Peter and Andrew immediately abandoned their nets and became his followers. Of James and John it is said that they also immediately abandoned boat and father to follow him.

In today's gospel this radical and immediate response is "fleshed out" in the story of St. Matthew. Jesus calls him just like the rest; Matthew responds just like the rest. But we then find Jesus at a party in Matthew's house! "While Jesus was at table in Matthew's home, many tax collectors and those known as sinners came to join Jesus." Apparently Jesus' call to apostolic poverty and holiness did not forbid Matthew from making use of his house and maintaining contact with his old friends.

Undoubtedly, there is a time to radically break with one's past. St. Paul says, "Those things I used to consider gain I have now reappraised as loss in the light of Christ." But Paul does not imply that we will break association with all non-Christian people. He says, "I wrote you in my letter not to associate with immoral persons. I was not speaking of association with immoral people in this world. . . . To avoid them, you would have to leave the world!" As Jesus says in today's gospel, "People who are in good health do not need a doctor; sick people do." Because Jesus himself went among "the sick," his opponents said, "This one is a glutton and a drunkard, a lover of tax collectors and those outside the law." We must break with the world, but we must genuinely love the people of the world. Jesus gave his life for the people of the world; we must do the same.

In the end, love will satisfy the radical demands of the gospel. Love calls us to poverty. Love calls us to holiness. Without love, poverty becomes an empty and life-draining curse. Without love, holiness degenerates into cold and heartless self-righteousness.

As St. Paul says, "If I speak with human tongues and angelic as well, but do not have love, I am a noisy gong, a clanging cymbal. If I have the gift of prophecy and, with full knowledge, comprehend all mysteries, if I have faith great enough to move mountains, but have not love, I am nothing. If I give everything I have to feed the poor and hand over my body to be burned, but have not love, I gain nothing." St. Paul says, "Love does not rejoice in what is wrong but rejoices in the truth." But he also says, "Love is patient, love is kind. . . . Love is never rude." James says, "Wisdom from above is first of all innocent. It is also peaceable, lenient, docile, rich in sympathy, and kindly deeds are its fruits." As Paul says aptly, "Love never wrongs the neighbors, hence love is the fulfillment of the law," and "There are in the end three things that last: faith, hope, and love, and the greatest of these is love."

Is our radical Christianity radical or fanatical? A fanatic fulfills the radical externals of poverty and holiness but does so without love. Love softens the edge of razor-sharp issues and changes the cutting edge from a sword that kills and maims into a surgical knife that heals. It brings us to the balance between no-compromise and the leniency of wisdom. Let us be radical, rather than fanatical, about the issues of poverty and moral purity. Let us learn the way of love.   ☐

Renew Us, Lord
Matthew 9:14-17 (13:Saturday)

People do not pour new wine into old wineskins. (v. 17)

When it comes to Spirit-led renewal, people often quote this Scripture in reference to old and established structures within the church. Some would say that the existing structures and teachings simply cannot accommodate the empowerment of the Spirit. How do Jesus' words about new wine relate to the church he established?

First, we can learn many things from what Jesus says to the Jews of his own day. He calls the leaders of the Jewish assembly "hypocrites," "blind guides," and "sons of hell." He says of their man-made laws, "They bind up heavy loads, hard to carry, to lay on other men's shoulders." Jesus speaks sharply about the hypocrisy of the scribes and Pharisees faulting them for failing to practice what they preached. But he also clearly implies that the existing man-made structures of Judaism were unable to house the "new wine" of the renewal he came to bring.

On the other hand, Jesus speaks of an extraordinary total obedience to the divinely ordained teaching office of the scribes and Pharisees. He says, "The scribes and Pharisees have succeeded Moses as teachers; therefore, do everything and observe everything they tell you. But do not follow their example." As to the old and established law of God in Scripture he says, "Do not think I have come to abolish the law and the prophets... not the smallest letter of the law, not the smallest part of the letter, shall be done away with until all comes true." Jesus clearly distinguished between what was of divine and what was of human origin. The divine he honored and obeyed. The human he challenged and often changed.

Eventually Christianity itself constituted an actual change in both the leadership and the law of the Jews, as it branched out to all the people and cultures of the world. It is from the experience of a developing church that Hebrews says, "Where there is a change in the priesthood, there is a necessary change in law." Even though "our Lord rose from the tribe of Judah, regarding which Moses said nothing about priests," the early church considered Jesus "high priest forever, according to the order of Melchizedek."

As the church spread beyond the realms of traditional Judaism to reach out to the Gentiles, the Jewish laws became less and less binding. Likewise, the leadership of the apostles and their successors became more central and primary, replacing the recognized leadership of the Jewish scribes and Pharisees. All this was due to the establishment of a new covenant by a new high priest to reach an entirely new group of people. As Hebrews concludes, "Jesus has obtained a more excellent ministry now, just as he is mediator of a better covenant, founded on better promises."

To say this does not imply that the New Testament church has no lasting structure. Jesus questioned the Jewish disciplines and man-made laws, but he also recognized the need for structure even within the new covenant assembly. He said, "How can the wedding guests go in mourning so long as the groom is with them?" But he also said, "When the day comes that the groom is taken away, then they will fast." Fasting is a discipline, an asceticism. It involves structure.

Jesus, indeed, chose leaders in the apostles, established sacraments for liturgical worship, and set down moral norms for the day-to-day life of his followers. He challenged the structures of the Jews as they related to the establishment of the new covenant, but he clearly established new structures for the protection and guidance of the new people of that covenant.

But is there today a new, new covenant? Is there a new leadership and a new structure for the church? Is this really a "new age"? There cannot be a change in leadership unless there is a change in the covenant—and vice-versa. "But when Christ came as high priest . . . he entered once for all." There is no new sacrifice so there is no new priesthood. The leadership of Jesus remains forever, so the apostolic leadership he himself established remains forever. This means that the essential apostolic structures and gospel laws of the new covenant church remain forever. They cannot change. There is no new Jesus, so there is no new church. If there is a new church, then there must be a new Jesus. Yet Jesus came "once for all."

Even so, we need to grow and develop. Paul says, "You form a building which rises on the foundation of the apostles and prophets, with Christ Jesus himself as the capstone." This analogy requires that we always build higher, toward something new. We build higher, on space which the church could not occupy in earlier ages. It had not yet risen high enough. Yet precisely because the church rose to the level it did, we can now build upon its experience and wisdom to something yet higher. And all this builds upon the foundation of the apostles and the prophets with Christ holding the whole thing together.

If we depart from this foundation and from the wisdom of the church through the ages, we are doomed to fail. If we move to the right or the left of the overall direction and design of the church, we will plummet to the ground, and shatter into useless pieces.

Throughout the history of the church many new charismatic movements and communities have emerged. Some have come and gone like the wind. Others have endured for the ages. Of course, there have been times when these movements of the Spirit were squelched by those in authority. Conversely, there have been times when these movements preempted the authority of the church and split the people of God in two. Sometimes these two extremes happen as a reaction to each other. But many other new movements have brought life to God's people while preserving the witness of the church through the ages. Praise God, the latter are more numerous!

How do we view the established church? Are our renewal movements working in union with or against the church that Jesus ordained? If we are part of the "establishment," how do we view renewal movements? Do we nurture or antagonize them? Only a Christ-like attitude can maintain unity in a church which calls itself Christian.   □

Never Too Proud to Ask
Matthew 9:18-26 (14:Monday)

"If only I can touch his cloak . . . I shall get well.". . . "Courage daughter! Your faith has restored you to health." (v. 21-22)

So many of us can relate to this gospel! The woman had been sick for twelve years. She had tried everything, yet could not be healed. As St. Mark says, "She had received treatment at the hands of doctors of every sort and had exhausted her savings in the process, yet she got no relief; on the contrary, she only grew worse." How many people we know in similar circumstances. Cancer and AIDS especially surface as incurable diseases in today's society.

I recall praying for a friend of mine with cancer. She had been treated in every way possible, yet the prognosis was still fatal. My friend was going to die. I can remember her weeping peacefully as she told me she had made a personal inventory of her life and had asked forgiveness from God for all her sins. She had attempted any personal reconciliation possible. She was ready to meet God. Yet she still asked God for healing. Like a child, she begged God for the continued gift of life. The example of the woman in today's gospel came to my mind. This courageous woman facing death was not too proud to ask God for a miracle.

I am reminded of Jesus in the garden of Gethsemane. He was facing the cross; he knew he was going to die. Yet he was not too proud to ask the Father for deliverance. He said, "My Father, if it is possible, let this cup pass from me. Still, let it be as you would have it, not as I." Jesus went on to die. Yet it was okay for him to ask for deliverance. If it was okay for Jesus, it should be okay for us.

In today's gospel Jesus heals the woman with the hemorrhage: "Your faith has restored you to health." In the case of Jesus, he went on to die. Yet it was the death on the cross itself that caused the greater healing: "Unless the grain of wheat falls to the ground and dies, it produces no fruit."

In the case of my friend, she went on to die. She is with Jesus now. Yet I feel that her life is spiritually closer to me now than ever before. Her life is a frequent reminder of faith, for she kept her faith in the stark face of death.

Do we face our hopeless situations with such faith? Are we too proud to ask for whatever we can get from God? Do we retain our false pride and security even in the face of the ultimate poverty of fatal sickness and destitution? Or, do we receive our crises as sources of healing and resurrection in our life? If we face death with faith, it becomes the doorway to eternal life.   □

Proclaim the Gospel
Matthew 9:32-38 (14:Tuesday)

The harvest is good but laborers are scarce. Beg the harvest master to send out laborers to gather his harvest. (v. 37-38)

The needs of this world are great; the issues are pressing. Never before have the choices been so clear: Be prolife or choose death; support military war and the unchecked buildup of nuclear arms, or seek peace; change our affluent life-style and preach the gospel to the poor or continue in our selfish indifference. Never before in history have our choices been so dictated by a loyalty either to Christ or to Antichrist.

Because of the clear consequences of our choices, the world is ripe for evangelism. When the need for gospel choices is so globally apparent, it becomes easier to proclaim the gospel. Because the need is obvious, presenting an answer becomes easy. The grey areas fast disappear in such an environment.

It is like proclaiming the gospel in a prison. A prison ministry is, in many ways, very easy. You do not have to convince a prisoner about the reality of sin. I guarantee you, inmates are intensely aware of the shortcomings of this world! All the evangelist must do is convince them that there is an answer.

So it is with our modern world. We live in a spiritual and moral prison. We all know it. We see it all around us. It is always with us. The problem is in breaking through the callousness of our insensitivity to sin. It is one thing to acknowledge sin; it is quite another to be grieved by it and truly sorry for it. As James says of this kind of callousness, "Do you believe that God is one? You are quite right. The demons believe that, and shudder." It is not enough to acknowledge sin. We must act upon this knowledge. We must begin to change.

The Scriptures speak of two ways of evangelizing. One is by speaking: "As you go, make this announcement: 'The reign of God is at hand!'" The other is by action: "Cure the sick, raise the dead, heal the lepers, expel demons." As Paul says, "How can they believe unless they have heard of him? And how can they hear unless there is someone to preach?" And as Jesus says, "Your light must shine before men so that they may see goodness in your acts." We need to proclaim by words, but words without action are cheap, while action without explanation is sometimes unclear. We need both in order to proclaim the gospel of Jesus Christ!

How do we proclaim the gospel today? Is it all words? Are we able to give the reason for our action? As Peter says, "Should anyone ask you the reason for this hope of yours, be ever ready to reply, but speak gently and respectfully." We must meet grave issues with radical response. But this response must be loving, balanced, and sure. Learn your faith and change your life-style. Then you will reap a great harvest for Jesus. □

Evangelizing within the Church
Matthew 10:1-7 (14:Wednesday)

Do not visit pagan territory and do not enter a Samaritan town. Go instead after the lost sheep of the house of Israel. (v. 5-6)

The Jews were the chosen people. This divine choice was not ignored by the Son of God, even though his ultimate mission was to the whole world. As Paul says, "There does not exist among you Jew or Greek, slave or freeman, male or female." Yet he speaks of the blessedness of the Jewish people: "Theirs were the adoption, the glory, the covenants, the law-giving, the worship, and the promises; theirs were the patriarchs, and from them came the Messiah." He says elsewhere, "What is the advantage, then, of being a Jew? . . . The answer is, much in every respect. First of all, the Jews were entrusted with words of God." Paul sees God revealed through nature to all people, but he sees the Jews as the keepers of God's word.

Likewise, whenever Paul went into an area to preach about Jesus, he always began in the synagogue. He followed the pattern of Jesus himself, who "continued his tour of all the towns and villages. He taught in their synagogues, he proclaimed the good news of God's reign, and he cured every sickness and disease." Even the people of the early church in Jerusalem "went to the temple area together every day, while in their homes they took their meals in common, praising God and winning the approval of all the people."

In today's world all of this can be applied to evangelism within the church. Throughout its history the church has seen countless communities raised up by the Spirit. They are all different, but they are all united by the church and minister the continual renewing work of the Holy Spirit to the church. Without the church the new communities would branch off into factions and divisions. But without the communities the church would often remain unrenewed by the Spirit.

Like the Jews, the church gave us the New Testament Scriptures, the sacraments, and the visible succession of apostolic leadership. Like the Jews, the church needs the prophetic, charismatic individuals and communities that "blow like the wind." Thus it is that the church is built "on the foundation of the apostles and prophets, with Christ Jesus himself as the capstone."

Unlike the case of the Jews who became Christians, there is no need for us to break away from the church. The break with the Jews was necessary for the early Christians, for there was a new covenant. As Paul says, "The law was our monitor until Christ came. . . . But now that faith is here, we are no longer in the monitor's charge." But with the new covenant church there is no need to break away. Such breaks only cause division, and as Paul says, "Let there be no factions." There is no *new* new covenant, so there is no need for a renewal structure outside the church. As Hebrews says, "When there is a change of priesthood, there is necessarily a change of law.... But Jesus ... has a priesthood which does not pass away."

Do we evangelize within the church? The word is there, Jesus is there, the structures are there. We need only awaken the multitude to the reality of the church they attend. Christ is the center of the church. Every doctrine, every sacrament, every church structure, is centered on him. All we need to do is proclaim the real meaning of the church and we will lead countless people to Christ. You do not need to leave the church in order to effectively bring Jesus to the world. □

Gospel Economics
Matthew 10:7-15 (14:Thursday)

The gift you have received, give as a gift. Provide yourselves with neither gold nor silver nor copper in your belts; ... no sandals, no walking staff. The workman, after all, is worth his keep. (v. 8-10)

Today's gospel speaks of Jesus' strange brand of ministry economics which has mystified both theologians and business managers for centuries. On the one hand, he seems to imply there should be no charge for ministry. On the other, it appears that he is saying that it is his right to expect that people should meet the ministers' needs. It seems that the minister should be destitute and poor. Yet it also seems that all his needs will be amply provided for.

Jesus does call his disciples to give up all their possessions: "None of you can be my disciple if he does not renounce all his possessions." Again he says "Sell what you have and give alms.... Wherever your treasure lies, there your heart will be." Yet he also says, "If you cannot be trusted with elusive wealth, who will trust you with lasting?" He calls his apostles to renounce all their wealth, yet Scripture and archeology tells us that Jesus' "base" for ministry in Galilee was Peter's house. Apparently, neither Peter nor Jesus felt the need to interpret these words literally.

Paul also had to apply the idealistic words of Christ in day to day ministry. He says of himself, "Up to this very hour we go hungry and thirsty, poorly clad, roughly treated, wandering about homeless. We work hard at manual labor." We know from the Acts of the Apostles that Paul worked with his own hands to support himself. In Corinth Paul took up lodging with a Jew named Aquila and his wife Priscilla "whose trade he had in common with them . . . they worked together as tentmakers." He said to the presbyters at Ephesus, "Never did I set my heart on anyone's silver or gold . . . these hands of mine have served both my needs and those of my companions." Even Paul had to take the lofty ideals of itinerant, apostolic poverty and translate them into the real world of supporting himself through either work or ministry.

But even Paul recognized that those who minister the gospel have the right to earn a living from the gospel, as long as the minister is content with gospel poverty. "Do we not have the right to marry a believing woman like the rest of the apostles and the brothers of the Lord and Cephas? Is it only myself and Barnabas who are forced to work for a living? What soldier in the field pays for his rations? Who plants a vineyard and does not eat of its yield? What shepherd does not nourish himself with the milk of his flock? . . . Likewise, the Lord himself ordered that those who preach the gospel should live by the gospel."

Of course, living by the gospel means one must also embrace the simplicity and poverty which keeps a minister from growing rich off the tithes and offerings of his people. As Paul says, "Such men value religion only as a means of personal gain. There is, of course, great gain in religion—provided one is content with a sufficiency . . . if we have food and clothing we have all that we need. Those who want to be rich are falling into a trap."

Paul deals even more directly about this "gospel ecomony" when dealing with marriage. "I should like you to be free of all worries. The unmarried man is busy with the Lord's affairs . . . but the married man is busy with the world's demands. . . . I have no desire to place restrictions on you, but I do want to promote what is good, what will help you to devote yourselves entirely to the Lord." As he reminds Timothy, "No soldier becomes entangled in the things of civilian life." So also should soldiers of Christ avoid entanglement in materialistic responsibility in order to be free to be drawn and guided by the "wind of the Spirit." If we are too tied down, this is impossible.

St. Francis understood this perfectly. He said that if we own property, we must take up arms and initiate litigation to defend it. Then we cannot be truly Christlike.

Of course, Paul speaks of a detachment and poverty of spirit that applies to all Christians, whether or not they are directly engaged in apostolic ministry. "From now on those with wives should live as though they had none; . . . buyers should conduct themselves as though they owned nothing, and those who make use of the world as though they were not using it, for the world as we know it is passing away."

Do we understand the economy of gospel poverty? The more we have the more we have to charge for our ministry. Then we cannot "give as a gift the gift we have received." Then we cannot really minister the gospel according to the gospel, nor "live by the gospel we preach." How many gospel preachers really understand this powerful "economy"? Until we do there will be no powerful revival. □

Words with Power
Matthew 10:16-23 (14:Friday)

You must be clever as snakes and innocent as doves. . . . The Spirit of your Father will be speaking in you. (v. 16, 20)

Do we try to explain our faith by God's power or by our own? St. Peter says, "Should anyone ask you . . . be ever ready to reply." But does this mean being always ready to argue, or to simply give witness?

Paul tells Timothy to teach but not to argue: "I charge you to preach the word, to stay with this task whether convenient or inconvenient—correcting, reproving, appealing—constantly teaching and never losing patience." Yet he also says, "Have nothing to do with senseless, ignorant disputations. As you well know, they only breed quarrels, and the servant of the Lord must not be quarrelsome but must be kindly toward all. He must be an apt teacher, patiently and gently correcting those who contradict him." Teach? Yes. Argue? No. Clever? Yes. Theological speculation? No.

We are called to give witness in the power of the Spirit. Simply state the reason why your life is different. If your life has not changed, your words will be meaningless. If your life has changed, your words will be charged with power.

Witnessing like this can only be done in the power of the Spirit. As Jesus said to the apostles, "You will receive power when the Holy Spirit comes down on you; then you are to be my witnesses." At Pentecost the outpouring of the Spirit caused each of them to "make bold proclamations as the Spirit prompted them." Suddenly a handful of uneducated, working-class fishermen became eloquent preachers! This was because it was the Spirit who spoke, not they themselves. As even the educated St. Paul said, "I did not come proclaiming God's testimony with any particular eloquence or 'wisdom.' My message had none of the persuasive force of 'wise' argumentation, but the convincing power of the Spirit."

Do we try to speak by our own power or by the power of the Spirit? Do we spend our time devising long speculative arguments to defend our particular theology or doctrine? Right or wrong, no theology will be powerfully defended without the Spirit. If we seek the power of the Spirit in our life, then our words will become instruments of testimony before the small as well as the great. Twelve simple men were used as instruments of God to permanently change the world. God is certainly willing to use you in the same way today!   □

Fear Not
Matthew 10:24-33 (14:Saturday)

Do not let them intimidate you. . . . What I tell you in darkness, speak in the light. What you hear in private, proclaim from the housetops. (v. 26, 27)

We must not be afraid to proclaim our faith in Christ. It might not always be popular; it might not always be easy. But we must not be afraid. We have been called to give witness to Jesus Christ before the world. As today's gospel says, "Whoever acknowledges me before men I will acknowledge before my Father in heaven. Whoever disowns me before men I will disown before my Father in heaven."

It is true that by proclaiming God's faith and morality to a sinful nation, we could be called into a civil court. Jesus said, "They will haul you into court.... You will be brought to trial before rulers and kings, to give witness before them and before the Gentiles on my account." It is also true that religious leaders will not always understand us: "They will flog you in their synagogues." But none of this should frighten us, for they can only harm the externals of our life. As Jesus said, "Do not fear those who deprive the body of life but cannot destroy the soul."

The Acts of the Apostles certainly proves the prophetic nature of Jesus' words. Peter is taken before the Sanhedrin, where he boldly says, "Better for us to obey God than men!" Stephen is not only brought before the Sanhedrin but illegally stoned to death. His last words were "Lord Jesus, receive my spirit.... Do not hold this sin against them."

Saul, after his conversion, even faced resistance within the church from those who said, "Unless you are circumcised according to Mosaic practice, you cannot be saved." But Paul "did not submit to them for a moment ... so that the truth of the gospel might survive intact." He even withstood Peter, "because he was clearly in the wrong."

Paul was taken before the Jewish Sanhedrin and before Roman commanders and governors. At each step he spoke with zeal and knowledge that confounded his questioners. Before the Sanhedrin he cleverly said, "Brothers, I am a Pharisee and was born a Pharisee. I find myself on trial now because of my hope in the resurrection of the dead." These words divided the Sanhedrin, half of which was made up of Pharisees, who believed in the resurrection, and half Sadducees, who did not.

Paul was a Roman citizen and not afraid to use the civil law to benefit the gospel. He asked the Roman commander who flogged him, "Is it legal to flog a Roman citizen without a trial?" King Agrippa even said to him, "A little more, Paul, and you will make a Christian out of me." Paul was shrewd and fearless. He fulfilled all of Jesus' words.

Paul speaks of his "many more labors and imprisonments," his "far more beatings and frequent brushes with death." He says, "Five times at the hands of the Jews I received forty lashes less one; three times I was beaten with rods; I was stoned once.... Leaving other sufferings unmentioned, there is that daily tension pressing on me, my anxiety for all the churches." And, "Persecution comes our way; we bear it patiently. We are slandered, and we try conciliation. We have become the world's refuse, the scum of all; that is the present state of affairs."

Through all this Paul is still driven to proclaim the gospel: "I am under compulsion and have no choice. I am ruined if I do not preach it." In the midst of persecution and pain he says, "We do not lose heart, because our inner being is renewed each day even though our body is being destroyed at the same time." As to church politics he says, "It is true, some preach Christ from motives of envy and rivalry.... What of it? All that matters is that ... Christ is being proclaimed!"

Today we face awesome challenges in our world: the prolife struggle, the arms race, fair distribution of the world's wealth, and the continued raping of mother earth by some greedy corporations, not to mention the breakdown of sexual morals and of the basic structure of the human family. Underneath all this is the need for personal conversion to Christ. Christians are called to speak the way of Jesus Christ in all these situations. We cannot be silent! Will we respond with the boldness of Peter, the shrewdness of Paul, and the gentleness of Stephen? As Jesus says, "You must be clever as serpents and gentle as doves." Are we willing to keep on proclaiming the good news of Jesus, even when we must face the same crucifixion that he and the apostles faced? If not, then we better not even open our mouths.   □

True and Lasting Peace
Matthew 10:34-11:1 (15:Monday)

Do not suppose that my mission on earth is to spread peace. My mission is to spread, not peace, but division. (v. 34)

Jesus never promises earthly peace. Any hope of our peace or social justice movements totally succeeding on this earth in the present age is in vain. Any theology that propagates the idea that we will somehow establish the Messianic kingdom of the so-called "millenium," where there is spiritual, political, and social peace, only fills people with false hope. Jesus never promises this kind of peace. It will only come after his return, and he will achieve it, not us.

In fact, Jesus foretells a time of great trouble and war before his coming. "You will hear of wars and rumors of wars.... Nation will rise against nation, one kingdom against another. . . . they will hand you over to torture and kill you. Indeed, you will be hated by all nations on my account."

To some extent, poverty is the reason we do not have peace. Scared of poverty, those who have much continue to oppress those who have nothing. Oppressed by poverty, those who have nothing resent, hate, and finally rise up in rebellion against those who have much. As James says, "Where do the conflicts and disputes among you originate? Is it not your inner cravings that make war within your members? What you desire you do not obtain, and so you resort to murder." Yet Jesus says, "The poor you will always have with you." Likewise, sin will be with us throughout this age. As Paul says, "All have sinned and fallen short of the glory of God." As long as poverty and sin are in this world together, we will not have total peace.

Yet Jesus does promise internal, spiritual peace. " 'Peace' is my farewell to you, my peace is my gift to you; I do not give it to you as the world gives peace." We may never see the external establishment of God's peace and social justice in this age, but that does not mean we will not know a deep abiding peace. Paul says, "Then God's own peace, which is beyond all understanding, will stand guard over your hearts and minds, in Christ Jesus."

This peace is a fruit of the Spirit, not the flesh. Paul says, "The fruit of the Spirit is love, joy, peace." To the church at Ephesus he says, "Make every effort to preserve the unity which has the Spirit as its origin and peace as its binding force." This peace is a matter of the heart and mind. It is something internal. It is a matter of the Spirit.

Does this mean we should not work for peace and social justice? Absolutely not! Jesus says, "Blessed are the peacemakers." Paul says, "If possible, live peaceably with everyone." Isaiah the prophet says, "Make justice your aim: Redress the wronged, hear the orphan's plea, defend the widow." Pope Paul VI says, "Peace is possible; therefore, it is a duty." Peace may not be promised, but it is possible if all will but follow God. As Jesus says, "It must be that the offenses come. But woe to those through whom the offenses come."

Peace might not be promised as a worldly reality, but it is a promised reality of the Spirit. And if it is a matter of the Spirit within, then it must manifest itself substantially in our external life. As James says, "Faith without works is dead."

Do we work for peace? Are we willing to let our dedication to God's peace separate us from those who persecute us for our ideals? On the other hand, do we sometimes fill ourselves with a false hope for total peace in the present world? Such peace is only possible in heaven. It is our final hope for lasting peace. As we sojourn here on earth we are still "pilgrims and strangers" as we pray, "Thy kingdom come, thy will be done on earth as it is in heaven." Let us work untiringly, but let us not entertain false hope, lest we grow disappointed and bitter and eventually turn away from God. God will fulfill his promise. Let us not presume to ask him for anything more.   □

Reform and Live!
Matthew 11:20-24 (15:Tuesday)

He began to reproach the towns where most of his miracles had been worked, with their failure to reform. . . . "I assure you, it will go easier for Tyre and Sidon than for you on the day of judgment." (v. 20, 22)

The key to Jesus' preaching is reform. "Reform your lives! The kingdom of heaven is at hand." We are not talking about a "feel good" faith. We are talking about a faith that will radically change our lives. Jesus' gospel calls us to change, and change now.

Sometimes this change is difficult. That is why Jesus uses such militant language about change: "If your right hand is your trouble, cut it off and throw it away!" Peter too uses aggressive language about reform: "So strip away everything vicious, everything deceitful: pretenses, jealousies, and disparaging remarks of any kind."

Granted, much of our change is almost effortless, because it is a love response to the love of God. As St. John says, "Love, then, consists in this: Not that we have loved God but that he has loved us and has sent his son as an offering for our sins." "Beloved, let us love one another because love is of God. . . . For God is love."

As Paul says, love is a fruit of the Holy Spirit. It appears almost naturally in a life where the Spirit has been firmly and surely implanted. "The fruit of the Spirit is love, joy, peace." But even with Paul the "gifts of the Spirit" must be sought. "Seek eagerly after love. Set your hearts on spiritual gifts." God might offer the gift as a total gift, but it takes a willful response to reach out and receive. This response requires change!

Peter spoke of such change as the first step in receiving the Spirit in a powerful way in our life. As the Acts of the Apostles says, "They asked Peter and the other apostles, 'What are we to do, brothers?' Peter answered, 'You must reform and be baptized, each one of you, in the name of Jesus Christ, that your sins may be forgiven; then you will receive the gift of the Holy Spirit.'" After this the account gives the description of the radical communal life of the church in Jerusalem, where not only "many wonders and signs were performed by the apostles" but also "those who believed shared all things in common." The true charismatic will be a person of radical change, and unless you are willing to radically change you cannot experience the full outpouring of the Spirit in your life.

What about us? Are we willing to radically reform, or do we still want to hang on to our comfortable way of life? Do we see the connection between gospel poverty and the work of the Spirit? Jesus requires that we reform our life from the bottom up—from the inside out through the Spirit, and from the outside in so the Spirit might flow freely. The Spirit will not move freely in our life until we are ready to give Jesus everything. This means we must be willing to change everything!

The towns of today's gospel received Jesus well enough. He spent much time in them: "He taught in their synagogues, he proclaimed the good news of God's reign, and he cured every sickness and disease." But after being given the marvelous gift of Jesus among them, they did not change!

Go to any of those cities today. All of them were thriving towns of industry. They were self-secure and full of life. Today not one of them is standing. All that is left are the archeological digs of scholars. No sounds of life are heard. No signs of a prospering metropolis remain. The time of their visitation is past. The time for reform is over.

Will you reach the same end? Or will you make the effort to truly change? Will you sit back smugly and rely on your Western affluence, or will you contemplate the end of the cities of today's gospel? Reform and you will live! Resist reform and you are dead already. ☐

The Spirit Teaches Us
Matthew 11:25-27 (15:Wednesday)

What you have hidden from the learned and clever you have revealed to the merest children. (v. 25)

So it is with the power of the gospel. Theologians fill the world; students fill our seminaries. All the world seems to clamor after knowledge, yet most of the world seems unable to arrive at the truth. As Paul says, "They make a pretense of religion but negate its power. Stay clear of them. It is such as these ... always learning but never able to teach a knowledge of the truth." He goes on elsewhere, "Warn certain people against teaching false doctrines ... which promote idle speculations rather than that training in faith which God requires." He speaks of such "knowledge" as "polemics and controversy." He finally warns Timothy, "Stay clear of worldly, idle talk and the contradictions of what is falsely called knowledge."

So it is today. Our seminaries are filled with young people seeking guidance in their faith. Instead they are often force-fed spiritual contradictions and human speculations that tear down their God-given faith. Woe to those who do this to God's little ones! As Paul says, "May condemnation fall on whoever it is that is unsettling you!"

But what is to be taught? How do we know the truth? Paul speaks of the ultimate goal of his teaching: "What we are aiming at in this warning is the love that springs from a pure heart, a good conscience, and sincere faith." He tells Timothy, "Train yourself for the life of piety," and, "Devote yourself to the reading of Scripture." He also says as an apostle to his son, "You, for your part, must remain faithful to what you have learned and believed, because you know who your teachers were."

Paul's basic teaching was the simple message of the birth, the cross, and the resurrection of Jesus Christ. "I determined that while I was with you I would speak of nothing but Jesus Christ and him crucified." There it is—simple knowledge of Scripture and apostolic tradition that leads to a healthy life of faith in Jesus Christ. That is what is needed. Nothing more, nothing less. Anything more is speculation. Anything less is incomplete. Finally, he says, "Guard the rich deposit of faith with the help of the Holy Spirit who dwells within us."

It is the Holy Spirit who leads the church into truth. As Isaiah says, "Who has directed the Spirit of the Lord, or has instructed him as his counselor? Whom did he consult to gain knowledge?" Without the Spirit no amount of study will lead us to God. With the Spirit our study becomes inspired, directed, and efficient. Without openness to the Spirit all our learning and teaching is powerless. As Paul says to the Corinthians, "I did not come proclaiming God's testimony with any particular eloquence or 'wisdom'. . . . My message and my preaching had none of the persuasive force of 'wise' argumentation, but the convincing power of the Spirit." With the Spirit our teaching is filled with power!

And what about us? Do we try to impress others with our knowledge, or do we let the power of the Spirit teach those who listen to us? We must have a relationship with God. As Jesus says in today's gospel, "No one knows the Son but the Father, and no one knows the Father but the Son—and anyone to whom the Son wishes to reveal him." Without the power of that love relationship we can know nothing about God, and despite all our study about God, we cannot teach anything!

We must proclaim, but with the Spirit we can proclaim clearly and simply in words that flow from an experienced relationship with Jesus, rather than from speculation. The Spirit then proclaims the mysteries with truth that cannot be contained in mere human speech. As Paul says, "What we utter is God's wisdom; a mysterious, a hidden wisdom. . . . Yet God has revealed this wisdom to us through the Spirit. . . . We speak of these, not in words of human wisdom, but in words taught by the Spirit."

How can we give what we do not possess? How can we teach in the Spirit if we have not really experienced the fullness of the Spirit in our life? The Spirit was given to us in Baptism and Confirmation, but we must actively reach out to receive if we are to daily experience his power.

Have you experienced the power of the Spirit lately? Priest or lay person, professor or student, it makes no difference. I ask you all the same question: Is the Holy Spirit powerfully active in your personal life? If not, all you need to do is ask. "The heavenly Father gives the Holy Spirit to those who ask him." Simply ask and actively receive, then you will proclaim the real power of God!   □

The Cross Gives Life
Matthew 11:28-30 (15:Thursday)

My yoke is easy and my burden light. (v. 30)

Jesus invites us to shoulder his burden if we want to find rest. The world is weary from carrying its own burden. It is parched from sojourning in the wilderness of sin. It needs to be refreshed. Jesus calls us to himself. He is the answer.

But what is the yoke and the burden of Christ if not the cross? Isaiah prophesies, "It was our infirmities that he bore, our sufferings that he endured. . . . Upon him was the chastisement that makes us whole, by his stripes we were healed. We had all gone astray like sheep, each following his own way; but the Lord laid upon him the guilt of us all. . . . He surrendered himself to death and was counted among the wicked; and he shall take away the sins of many, and win pardon for their offenses." As Paul says, "Christ has delivered us from the power of the law's curse by himself becoming a curse for us, as it is written, 'Accursed is anyone who is hanged on a tree.'" This all happened on the cross.

But how could the cross be "easy" and "light"? Sirach speaks of the burden of the discipline involved in the study of God's wisdom: "My son, from your youth embrace discipline; thus will you find wisdom with greying hair. . . . Put your feet into her fetters, and your neck under her yoke. Stoop your shoulders and carry her, and be not irked at her bonds. . . . Afterward you will find rest in her, and she will become your joy. Her fetters will be your throne of majesty; her bonds, your purple cord." It sounds almost as if today's gospel is directly influenced by this Old Testament Scripture on wisdom!

But Paul speaks of a more personalized freedom in the cross, something more than the mere rewards of hard labor: "I have been crucified with Christ, and the life I live now is not my own; Christ is living in me." Paul joined with Christ on the cross so that his whole life—body, soul, and spirit—might be made new by Christ's power rather than his own.

This sharing in the life of Christ means sharing in the work of Christ on the cross. We are "coheirs" and coworkers in bringing redemption. As Paul mystically says, "In my own flesh I fill up what is lacking in the sufferings of Christ for the sake of his body, the church." And to the Galatians, "Let no man trouble me, for I bear the brand marks of Jesus in my body."

If we want to bring healing to others, we must be willing to share in their pain, or else we cannot call our healing Christian, says St. Paul. We must be willing to die with the dying in order to bring them new life in Christ. As Paul says of the Jews, "I could even wish to be separated from Christ for the sake of my brothers, my kinsmen the Israelites."

"The fruit of the Spirit is love, joy, peace. . . . Those who belong to Christ Jesus have crucified their flesh with its passions and desires. Since we live by the Spirit, let us follow the Spirit's lead."

If we die we will also rise. Death on the cross brings resurrection! Do we see the cross as a source of life or as a source of pain? Do we seek to embrace it out of love, or do we run from it out of fear? Are we willing to embrace it willingly so that others might be raised to new life? If we do not see the miraculous healings of the Spirit active in and through our life, perhaps it is because we do not actively embrace the cross. If we are not at rest and peace, perhaps it is because we have not yet died. □

Our Rest Is in Him
Matthew 12:1-8 (15:Friday)

"It is mercy I desire and not sacrifice". . . . The Son of Man is indeed Lord of the sabbath. (v. 7-8)

The disciples were in clear violation of the laws of the Jews. God had said in the law, "Remember to keep holy the sabbath day. Six days you may labor and do all your work, but the seventh day is the sabbath of the Lord, your God." He also said, "On that day you must rest even during the seasons of plowing and harvesting." Even of the miracle of the manna from heaven and its collection Scripture says, "On the sixth day they gathered twice as much food. . . . 'You may either bake or boil the manna as you please, but whatever is left, put away and keep for tomorrow!'" The law prohibited all buying and selling on the sabbath. It even prohibited the lighting of a fire to cook a meal!

The disciples, as poor men, had rightly gathered grain from others' fields. Scripture says, "When you reap the harvest in your field and overlook a sheaf there, you shall not go back and get it; let it be for the alien, the orphan, and the widow," and, "When you go through your neighbor's grainfield, you may pluck some of the ears with your hand, but do not put a sickle to your grain." The law was full of such injunctions concerning the rights of the alien and the poor. Yet the disciples were in clear violation of the laws concerning the sabbath.

A deeper reading of Scripture points out a less stringent approach to the law. Jesus points out, "The priests on temple duty can break the sabbath rest without incurring guilt." And concerning David when he was fleeing Saul, "He ate the holy bread, a thing forbidden to him and his men or anyone other than priests." The law said, "It shall belong to Aaron and his sons, who must eat it in a sacred place," yet David and his men ate this sacred bread even though they were not priests.

Here Jesus points out the deeper meaning of the law. People do not exist only to serve the law. The law exists for people, to bring them to God. The law manifests God's holiness and his mercy. To lose sight of this is to keep the law in vain.

But Jesus claims another reason for the disciples' actions. It is the divine authority of Jesus himself. True, they are in obedience to the heart of the law. But they are also obedient to the Giver of the laws. Jesus is "Lord of the sabbath." It is "the sabbath of the Lord, your God." Here Jesus is calling himself God!

Do we see Jesus as Lord, as God? In fulfilling the religious laws of the church, do we look to their spiritual heart, or do we only see the externals? Do we really appreciate the rest and holiness of a weekly sabbath, or do we work nonstop?

Jesus wants to lead us into a spiritual rest. As Hebrews says, "A sabbath rest still remains for the people of God. And he who enters into God's rest rests from his own work as God did from his." The sabbath of the disciples of Jesus brings inner peace. It is deeper than mere externals. □

A Foolish Approach?
Matthew 12:14-21 (15:Saturday)

He will proclaim justice to the Gentiles. He will not contend or cry out, nor will his voice be raised in the streets. (v. 18-19)

Isn't this a contradiction? He proclaims justice, yet he does not do what most peace and justice marchers do? How can he proclaim justice if he does not raise his voice to contend injustice? How will he bring his cause to the people if he does not cry out in the streets?

Jesus defies all our modern definitions. He goes much deeper than the movements that try to solve the social ills of our time. He leads by following. He overcomes by submitting. He resists by not resisting. This is contrary to all secular approaches to establishing justice. It is mystical, and it can only be perceived and preached by those who operate in the Spirit. Yet its effects are vast! As Paul says, "The spiritual man can appraise everything, though he himself can be appraised by no one." The world might not see the wisdom of our approach, but all the world is affected by it!

All of creation was affected by the death and resurrection of Jesus, yet this took place in an unimportant, out-of-the-way, Mideastern province of the Roman Empire two thousand years ago! As Paul says to the Colossians, "It pleased God . . . by means of him to reconcile everything in her person, both on earth and in the heavens, making peace through the blood of his cross." And to the Romans, "Indeed, the whole created world eagerly awaits the revelation of the sons of God."

The way of Jesus Christ and his followers might seem ineffectual, but it affects all of creation. The way of nonresistance might seem to fail, but it really succeeds better than any other way. Granted, it takes longer; we do not always see immediate results. But results are longer-lasting when they are achieved according to the full example of Jesus Christ.

What was this way of establishing justice? Peter says, "He did no wrong; no deceit was found in his mouth. When he was insulted, he returned no insult. When he was made to suffer, he did not counter with threats. Instead, he delivered himself up to the One who judges justly. In his own body he brought your sins to the cross, so that all of us, dead to sin, could live in accord with God's will." □

Seek God, Not His Gifts
Matthew 12:38-42 (16:Monday)

An evil and unfaithful age is eager for a sign! (v. 39)

Are we anything more than "sign seekers"? Do we seek the gifts or the Giver of the gifts? Many of us get all excited about healings and prophecies and apparitions in other lands. But as soon as the excitement of these wear off, we find our faith waning and our life headed back to our old secular ways. Is this really faith? Is this what God seeks to accomplish through such extraordinary graces?

Jesus recognizes that miracles and signs give witness to God's power. He says, not without some exasperation, "Unless you people see signs and wonders, you do not believe." He says to the disciples of John the Baptist, "Go back and report to John what you hear and see: the blind recover their sight, cripples walk, lepers are cured, the deaf hear, dead men are raised to life, and the poor have the good news preached to them." He goes on concerning John, "Yet I have testimony greater than John's, namely, the works the Father has given me to accomplish. These very works which I perform testify on my behalf that the Father has sent me." As the Acts of the Apostles says, "Jesus the Nazarene was a man whom God sent to you with miracles, wonders, and signs as his credentials."

Signs also accompanied the apostles and the early church: "A reverent fear overtook them all, for many wonders and signs were performed by the apostles." Jesus himself promised, "Signs like these will accompany those who have professed their faith." Even of the controversial gift of tongues, given primarily to upbuild those who already believe, Paul admits, "The gift of tongues is a sign, not for those who believe but for those who do not believe." Signs and wonders are given by God to establish and strengthen saving faith!

But what of today's gospel? Here Jesus says sign seeking is done by an evil and faithless generation. Paul says, "Jews demand 'signs' and Greeks look for 'wisdom,' but we preach Christ crucified—a stumbling block to the Jews, and an absurdity to the Gentiles." At the trial of Jesus it was the faithless Herod who "was hoping to see him work some miracle." The only miracle Jesus would perform would be one greater than any other—resurrection from the dead!

The story of Thomas might help us. In order to strengthen Thomas's faith in his resurrection, Jesus appeared to him and said, "Take your finger and examine my hands. Put your hand into my side. Do not persist in your unbelief, but believe!" Then he said, "You became a believer because you saw me. Blest are they who have not seen and have believed."

Jesus gives us signs and wonders because he knows we are weak. He loves us, so he meets us where we are. Yet he highly commends those whose faith is so strong that they do not need such signs in order to keep believing.

Do we have such faith? Is it enough to simply remember the powerful salvation God has repeatedly brought into our life, or must we be constantly reminded? An adult remembers and calmly goes forward; a child must be constantly reminded and prodded to keep on going. Let us have the faith of a mature Christian. Let us be children no longer.

As Paul says, "Let us, then, go beyond the initial teaching about

Christ and advance to maturity." Concerning spiritual gifts he concludes, "Do not be childish in your outlook. Be like children as far as evil is concerned, but in mind be mature." We must have the childlike humility to seek the gifts given to us by a loving Father. But demanding signs and wonders of God is not childlike humility; it is more like a temper tantrum of a spoiled child. Be childlike in seeking; do not be childish in demanding signs. □

Family Matters
Matthew 12:46-50 (16:Tuesday)

Whoever does the will of my heavenly Father is brother and sister and mother to me. (v. 50)

In today's gospel Jesus' earthly family comes to the crowded scene of his active ministry to talk to him. Matthew and Luke depict the family as rather neutral, so Jesus' response could well apply to them also. Mark's Gospel is not quite so bland. It says that the crowds gathering around Jesus and the disciples made "it impossible for them to get any food whatever. When his family heard of this they came to take charge of him, saying, 'He is out of his mind.'" John's Gospel says, "As a matter of fact, not even his brothers had much confidence in him." Apparently Jesus' words here are not so much a praise of his earthly family's faith as a contrast between their doubt and the faith of his other followers. It is somehow comforting to know that even Jesus had to deal with family tensions!

Who is this earthly family of Jesus Christ? Tradition gives two options as to who these brothers were. The oldest tradition claims that Mary, having made a vow of virginity at an early age, was taken under the protection of an elderly Joseph when she came of age to marry. He had other children from a previous marriage, so they became the half-brothers and half-sisters of Jesus. The second theory is that of St. Jerome, who claimed that these "brothers" were what we call cousins, following the Old Testament example of calling cousins one's brothers and sisters.

A third theory is that Mary was not always a virgin but had relations with Joseph after the birth of Jesus and bore other children through natural intercourse. This theory was rejected by the Catholic church, for it went contrary to the apostolic tradition about Mary's perpetual virginity. Probably one of the first two theories is correct, for both of them are consistent with apostolic tradition and Scripture.

Presumably these blood relatives of Jesus converted to the faith and became his followers. Paul calls the apostle James, who was the first bishop of Jerusalem, "the brother of the Lord" and says of those who minister in the early church, "Do we not have a right to marry a believing woman like the rest of the apostles and the brothers of the Lord and Cephas?" Paul says that Jesus actually "appeared to James, and then to all the apostles" in one of his many resurrection appearances. I guess this would make believers out of his doubting brothers!

Our natural families can be incorporated into the larger family of God, but this does not happen without faith. The spiritual family must come first. Jesus says, "If anyone comes to me without turning his back on his father and mother, his wife, and his children, his brothers and sisters, indeed even his very self, he cannot be my follower." Yet he promises a new spiritual family; "I give you my word, there is no one who has given up home, brothers or sisters, mother or father, children or property, for me and the gospel who will not receive in this present age a hundred times as many homes, brothers and sisters, mothers, children and property."

As Jesus says in today's gospel, every believer becomes our brother or sister, and every mother becomes our mother in "mother church." As we are part of the church, we ourselves become the bride of Christ. Jesus becomes our brother, and Mary becomes both sister and mother to us all, to the whole church! This is the great and abundant love relationship we have with Jesus Christ. It brings us into the greatest possible love relationship any human being can have, both with God and with the people he created and redeemed in Christ. In terms of family, no fuller and more complete family can be experienced on earth outside the full and wonderful family we now call the church.

How do we deal with our earthly families? Do we compromise the gospel in order to keep peace? Or does our sometimes fanatical faith create unnecessary problems at home?

Jesus says, "Do not suppose that my mission on earth is to spread peace. My mission is to spread, not peace, but division. I have come to set a man at odds with his father, a daughter with her mother, a daughter-in-law with her mother-in-law: in short, to make a man's enemies those of his own household." Yet the Scriptures also say of a church leader, "He must be a good manager of his own household, keeping his children under control without sacrificing his dignity; for if a man does not know how to manage his own house, how can he take care of the church of God?" Finding the proper balance between these two Scriptures can be challenging, but the Lord will lead us to the truth. □

Listen and Learn
Matthew 13:1-9 (16:Wednesday)

Great crowds gathered around him. . . . He addressed them at length in parables. (v. 2, 3)

Do we grow weary when the preacher begins to speak to us at length? Many of us allow our preachers only a few minutes to deliver their homilies or sermons. It sounds like the time allotted to fix instant food rather than to deliver the eternal word of God, "bread of the finest wheat." Then we complain because we only have an "instant" understanding of our Christian or Catholic faith. Good food requires time to prepare. You cannot really have one without the other.

Jesus spoke at length both to the crowds and privately to the apostles. The apostles also spoke at length. All through the Acts of the Apostles are the eloquent, Spirit-led discourses that Stephen, James, Peter, and Paul spoke to the church. At Pentecost "they began to make bold proclamations as the Spirit prompted them." The church in Jerusalem "devoted themselves to the apostles' instruction." This is quite amazing considering how uneducated the apostles were in religious matters. They were not rabbis, yet the people listened to them because they were anointed by the Spirit.

The question is, how devoted are we as listeners? Also, how

Spirit-filled are the proclamations of our preachers? We often have preachers who are educated in seminary but not fully anointed by the Spirit. Likewise, we often have anointed preachers but spiritually dead congregations. Let's look at a humorous story about Paul to find the balance.

At one point Paul began speaking in the morning during "the breaking of the bread." Then, "because he intended to leave the next day, he kept speaking until midnight." This means that Paul preached for more than twelve straight hours! Sure enough, a "young lad named Eutychus . . . became drowsier and drowsier. He finally went sound asleep, and fell from the third story window to the ground." Paul preached so long that the boy actually died!

Yet Paul, because he was anointed by the Spirit in all of this, worked a healing in the boy, and he was raised to life. What did Paul do then? "Afterward Paul went upstairs again, broke bread, and ate. Then he talked for a long while—until his departure at dawn. To the great comfort of the people, they were able to take the boy away alive." After all that, Paul kept on preaching! I wonder if the people were relieved because of Paul's preaching or because he finally stopped? Anyway, because of Paul's preaching, the boy barely got away with his life!

Was Paul not in the Spirit, or was the boy not attentive enough? I don't think we can really say one way or the other. In any case, the Spirit worked through them both. Salvation was manifested through both the preaching and the healing ministry of Paul. Perhaps Paul kept his sermons a little shorter from then on.

Are we really devoted to the apostolic instruction given us by our preachers? Really, how many of us would not be a little perturbed if our preachers went on too long on Sunday morning? Let's give them the opportunity to talk a little too long if they need to. Then perhaps we might find them more inspired and excited about what they have to say. There is nothing more uninspiring than preaching to a cold and even hostile congregation.

Are those of us who preach really inspired by the Holy Spirit in our words? To preachers I would quote my patron, St. Francis: "I advise and admonish the friars that in their preaching, their words be examined and chaste. They should aim only at the advantage and spiritual good of their listeners, . . . because our Lord himself kept his words short on earth."   □

Mysteries Revealed
Matthew 13:10-17 (16:Thursday)

I use parables when I speak to them because they look but do not see, they listen but do not hear or understand. (v. 13)

Did Jesus use parables to make his teaching clearer or to make it more mysterious? Most people think parables make spiritual teachings clearer and more understandable to the common listener. Ironically, Jesus says he taught in parables in order to keep the meaning obscure! In Luke's Gospel he says, "To you the mysteries of the reign of God have been confided, but to the rest in parables, that 'seeing they may not perceive.'" Luke's account has Jesus almost intentionally clouding his real meaning by using parables!

Today's account from Matthew is more passive. Yet both accounts bring out the mystical role of Jesus in helping us understand the spiritual realities of his teaching. Both Gospels relate that Jesus personally explained the parables to the disciples. Both include the obscure saying of Jesus related to the parables, "To the man who has, more will be given until he grows rich; the man who has not will lose what little he had."

Is Jesus speaking of material riches? No, I do not think so. He is speaking of wisdom and understanding. Wisdom says, "I deemed riches nothing in comparison with her, nor did I liken any priceless gem to her; because all gold, in view of her, is a little sand, and before her, silver is to be accounted mire."

But how do we obtain wisdom? James says, "If any of you is without wisdom, let him ask it from the God who gives generously and ungrudgingly to all, and it will be given him." Wisdom is a gift from God, a gift of the Holy Spirit. Isaiah says, "The Spirit of the Lord shall rest upon him: a Spirit of wisdom and of understanding." As Paul says, "God has revealed this wisdom to us through the Spirit."

The wisdom to understand Jesus' parables cannot be learned through natural knowledge. The apostles' interpretation of Old Testament prophecy was not always literal; it was allegorical at best. The early church continued this approach, especially through saints like Augustine. Understanding this allegorical teaching is a gift from God's Spirit. Paul says, "No one knows what lies at the depths of God but the Spirit of God. The Spirit we have received is not the world's spirit, but God's Spirit. . . . We speak of these, not in words of human wisdom but in words taught by the Spirit, thus interpreting spiritual things in spiritual terms. The natural man does not accept what is taught by the Spirit of God. . . . The spiritual man . . . can appraise everything, though he himself can be appraised by no one."

If we think we have the wisdom to understand Jesus' parables just because we are educated, then we will lose what little understanding we have. If we have understanding through the Spirit, be we educated or uneducated according to human standards, our wisdom will increase to the point of great spiritual riches.

Do we seek the guidance of the Spirit in understanding Jesus? Jesus calls the Spirit the "Spirit of truth, [who] will guide you into all truth." The great saints sought this allegorical understanding of all Jesus' teachings; they preferred it to the mere intellectual understanding of Scripture. Seek the Spirit in your life, then Jesus' obscure teachings will become clear. Then Jesus will also say of you, "Blest are your eyes because they see and blest are your ears because they hear. I assure you, many a prophet and many a saint longed to see what you see but did not see it, to hear what you hear but did not hear it." Let us be eternally grateful that Jesus has given us of his Spirit, to personally teach us of the kingdom of God! □

Life-giving Meditations
Matthew 13:18-23 (16:Friday)

But what was sown on good soil is the man who hears the message and takes it in. He it is who bears a yield of a hundred or sixty or thirtyfold.
(v. 23)

We hear the word of God at every liturgy. At every mass we hear the gospel solemnly proclaimed. At every other kind of liturgy the various parts of Scripture are intentionally included. Catholics and high churches probably hear more of the Scriptures than any other Christian body of believers. Yet we tend to know the Scriptures less. Why?

The Scriptures must be meditated on, not just read. The psalmist says, "Happy the man who ... meditates on his law day and night." But we cannot really meditate on the Scriptures unless we love the Scriptures.

Paul says, "All Scripture is inspired of God and is useful for teaching—for reproof, correction, and training in holiness so that the man of God may be fully competent and equipped for every good work." He says in his letter to the Romans, "Everything written before our time was written for our instruction, that we might derive hope from the lessons of patience and the words of encouragement in the Scriptures." This is not just dry study. This is a meditation that has definite effects in our daily spiritual life.

Paul calls the Scriptures "the source of the wisdom which through faith in Jesus Christ leads to salvation." Notice that the Scriptures alone are not enough. They must be combined with faith in Jesus Christ. Then they come to life. St. Bonaventure says that the study of Scripture without the faith that comes from the Spirit will never lead us to its real meaning. Read without faith and the Scriptures remain only dead letters.

Francis of Assisi says, "St. Paul tells us, 'The letter kills, but the Spirit gives life' (2 Cor 3:6). A man has been killed by the letter when he wants to know quotations only so that people will think he is very learned and he can make money to give to his relatives and friends. A religious has been killed by the letter when he has no desire to follow the Spirit of the Sacred Scripture, but wants to know what it says only so that he can explain it to others. On the other hand, those have received life from the Spirit of Sacred Scripture who, by their word and example, refer to the most high God, to whom belongs all good, all that they know or wish to know, and do not allow their knowledge to become a source of self-complacency."

As Sirach says of the scribe, "[He] devotes himself to the study of the law of the Most High. . . . He treasures the discourses of famous men. . . . He studies obscure parables. . . . He is in attendance on the great. . . . He travels among the peoples of foreign lands." Most of all, "His care is to seek the Lord his Maker, . . . to open his lips in prayer, to ask pardon for his sins.

Then, if it pleases the Lord Almighty, he will be filled with the spirit of understanding."

Do we really take the time to meditate on Scripture? Is the time we take quality time, or just leftover time when we are tired and exhausted? If we take the time, do we really pray the Scriptures in humility, or do we still study out of vanity and pride? If we pray the Scriptures as God's personal word to us as individuals and as a church, they will affect our lives. If we really fill our mind with the Scriptures, they will transform our lives. As Sirach says, "The root of all conduct is the mind." Meditation on Scripture helps us in the "spiritual renewal of the mind," as Paul calls it. Read and pray. Then let your life be transformed.   □

The Power to Judge
Matthew 13:24-30 (16:Saturday)

"No," he replied, "pull up the weeds and you might take the wheat along with them. Let them grow together until harvest." (v. 29-30)

So it is within the church. There is the good and the bad, the wheat and the weeds. Some people are very sincere, others are less sincere. All we can ask for is a sign of repentance, a profession of faith, and the desire to receive the sacraments. If people willingly come forward with all of these, who are we to judge their souls and tell them they don't really have faith in Jesus?

The church has been given the power to judge to a certain degree. Jesus tells the apostles, "If you forgive men's sins, they are forgiven them; if you hold them bound, they are held bound." Jesus first gave this power to St. Peter: "I for my part declare to you, you are 'Rock,' and on this rock I will build my church, and the jaws of death shall not prevail against it. I will entrust to you the keys of the kingdom of heaven. Whatever you declare bound on earth shall be bound in heaven; whatever you declare loosed on earth shall be loosed in heaven." He later gave this power to the other apostles.

Peter, therefore, judges Ananias and Sapphira in the Jerusalem church, discerning that "you let Satan fill your heart so as to make you lie to the Holy Spirit." In response to Peter's pronouncement, both Ananias and Sapphira fell over dead! Paul judges the morality of the habitually incestuous man at Corinth and says, "I hand him over to Satan for the destruction of his flesh, so that his spirit may be saved on the day of the Lord." He later instructs the church at Corinth to receive him back into their fellowship, "so that he may not be crushed by the great weight of sorrow."

These church judgments can only be carried out in grave matters regarding faith and morality. Anything more than this comes dangerously close to transgressing Jesus' solemn warning, "If you want to avoid judgment, stop passing judgment." As James says, "Not many of you should become teachers; you should realize that those of us who do so will be called to stricter account." And Peter says to the church leaders, "Be examples to the flock, not lording it over those assigned to you, so that when the chief Shepherd appears you will win for yourselves the unfading crown of glory."

We see that both good and bad existed even in the early church. Paul says to Titus, "There are many irresponsible teachers, especially from among the Jewish converts. . . . These must be silenced. They are upsetting whole families by teaching things they have no right to teach." But while Paul fights to keep right belief and orthodoxy, he also realizes that not all will do things just as he does: "It is true, some preach Christ from motives of envy and rivalry. . . . What of it? All that matters is that in any and every way, whether from suspicious motives or genuine ones, Christ is being proclaimed!" As Jesus said concerning the man who proclaimed him but did not join the apostolic band of disciples, "Do not stop him, for any man who is not against you is on your side."

What about us? Do we try to judge those we don't agree with in the church? Do we secretly pray that the pope and the bishops will make official pronouncements about a doctrine, when, in fact, all we want is to be proven right, to win? We must not hate even those who teach heresy. We must love them, and love them from our heart. As James says, "Wisdom from above is first of all innocent. It is also peaceable, lenient, docile, rich in sympathy." Judgment should come only after docile leniency, and then only through the pope and the bishops who have been given the power of the keys as successors to Peter and the apostles. Anything more than this incurs the risk of divine judgment of our soul, through our own human judgment of another. ☐

Be Great in the Spirit
Matthew 13:31-35 (17:Monday)

He proposed still another parable: "The reign of God is like a mustard seed".... He offered them still another image: "The reign of God is like yeast." (v. 31, 33)

Today Jesus tells us to begin small. Our modern world says, "Big is better." Capitalism must, by its nature, either get bigger or die. Corporations start out as comfortable, small businesses but grow into megapowers that often control the very people who run them. Ministries too start out with pure spiritual motives but often grow into large spiritual empires which must face the real problems of cash flow and corporate priorities. Bigger ministry needs more employees, more equipment—and all this must be paid for and maintained. Soon, instead of a ministry being motivated by the Spirit, it is motivated by one thing alone: It is motivated by money.

In today's parables Jesus tells us to begin small in ministry. The mustard seed "is the smallest seed of all." The yeast is only a small part of the dough. Elsewhere Jesus says, "Anyone among you who aspires to greatness must serve the rest." Likewise, "If you can trust a man in little things, you can also trust him in greater." He underlays all of this with his teaching of renunciation: "None of you can be my disciple if he does not renounce all his possessions."

The problem, however, is not in being big; it is in *desiring* worldly greatness and power. In today's parables greatness is, in fact, achieved. The mustard seed "when full-grown . . . is the largest of plants." Undoubtedly there will be problems with keeping "the world" out, for "it becomes so big a shrub that the birds of the sky come and build their nests in its branches." The yeast causes the whole mass of dough to rise. The ministry born of the Spirit will grow great. As Jesus said, "To the man who has, more will be given until he grows rich; the man who has not will lose what little he has."

There is, however, a difference between greatness in the world and greatness in the Spirit. John says, "Have no love for the world, nor the things that the world affords." What is of the world? "Carnal allurements, enticements for the eye, the life of empty show—all these are from the world." When a ministry gets showy, it has crossed the line from the Spirit to the world. When it expends more energy in externals than internals, it is in serious trouble.

How many of our ministries have crossed the line between the Spirit and the world? Is our greatness of the Spirit or of the flesh? "The flesh is at enmity with God," says Paul. "If anyone loves the world, the Father's love has no place in him," says John. If we begin in the Spirit, we will grow to greatness. We will undoubtedly have to deal with the world. "I do not ask you to take them out of the world, but to guard them from the evil one," prays Christ. Let us guard today against the evil one's corruption of our ministry and our life. □

The Purification of the Church
Matthew 13:36-43 (17:Tuesday)

Explain to us the parable of the weeds in the field. (v. 36)

The parables of Matthew 13 can all be applied to life in the church. These parables are extremely helpful, for life in the church can be both our greatest support and our greatest trial as Christians. These parables help reconcile this seeming contradiction.

In this particular parable Jesus tells us that "the good seed" consists of "the citizens of the kingdom. The weeds are the followers of the evil one and the enemy who sowed them is the devil." This means that the children of God and the children of the devil live together in the world. Jesus tells us not to even try to pull out the weeds, the children of the devil. He says, "Pull up the weeds and you might take wheat along with them. Let them grow together until harvest." At the harvest they will be separated by the angels of God, who carry out the perfect and just judgment of God.

Paul speaks of the church as pure, yet he recognizes the tension between the "already" and the "not yet." He knows all too well the human problems of the divinely inspired church, which must reside in a world filled with evil. He says, "Christ loved the church. He gave himself up for her to make her holy, purifying her in the bath of water by the power of the word, to present to himself a glorious church, holy and immaculate, without stain or wrinkle or anything of that sort." And again, "I have given you in marriage to one husband, presenting you as a chaste virgin to Christ."

But he goes on, "My fear is that, just as the serpent seduced Eve by his cunning, your thoughts may be corrupted and you may fall away from your sincere and complete devotion to Christ." He even mentions false teachers and false apostles among the church: "Such men are false apostles. They practice deceit in their disguise as apostles of Christ. And little wonder! Even Satan disguises himself as an angel of light." Paul clearly recognizes the human problems of false teaching and the division it causes in the church. As Jesus prophesied, "Many will come to impersonate me. . . . False prophets will rise in great numbers and mislead many, . . . performing signs and wonders so great as to mislead even the chosen if that were possible."

Jesus also recognized the need for at least some church discipline. He gave the power of the keys to Peter and the apostles: "Whatever you declare bound on earth shall be bound in heaven; whatever you declare loosed shall be loosed in heaven." Paul exercised this authority with the incestuous man in Corinth: "I hand him over to Satan for the destruction of his flesh, so that his spirit may be saved on the day of the Lord." Notice, however, in his second letter he continues, "the punishment already inflicted by the majority on such a one is enough; you should now relent and support him so that he may not be crushed by too great a weight of sorrow."

The discipline of the church has always been rather lenient. The requirements for membership are minimal. And any discipline eventually gives way to forgiveness, after appropriate signs of repentance and change. About all we can ask of our members is a public profession of faith, a desire to receive Jesus in the celebration of the sacraments, and a life free of habitual and

malicious immorality. Anything more than this comes dangerously close to exercising the judgment that can only be justly and
perfectly accomplished by God.

Do we judge our brothers and sisters prematurely? Only God
can judge the heart. When we judge, we can do much harm.
Sometimes we will judge incorrectly and uproot innocent followers of Jesus by mistake. Let us judge only as Christ has
allowed. Anything more than that is sin. □

Hidden Wisdom
Matthew 13:44-46 (17:Wednesday)

*The reign of God is like a buried treasure which a man found in a field.
He hid it again, and rejoicing at his find went and sold all he had and
bought that field.* (v. 44)

So it is with the church. Sometimes the treasure of the church
seems very evident. At other times its spiritual wealth seems to
have gotten buried somewhere. Yet by faith one must forsake all
else in the world. Then we are able to uncover the treasure.

The treasure of the church is both seen and hidden, visible and
invisible. Jesus says, "You can tell a tree by its fruit.... Any sound
tree bears good fruit, while a decayed tree bears bad fruit." Paul
also speaks of the visible fruit of the Spirit: "The fruit of the Spirit
is love, joy, peace, patient endurance, kindness, generosity, faith,
mildness, and chastity."

But the spiritual dimension of the church is also invisible. This
wisdom is a hidden wisdom of the Spirit: "What we utter is God's
wisdom; a mysterious, a hidden wisdom. None of the rulers of this
age knew the mystery."

The unity of the church is a matter of both the visible and the
invisible. The church is made up of visible people who are
governed by a visible apostolic leadership: "You form a building
which rises on the foundation of the apostles and prophets." Yet
its unity is also a matter of the invisible working of the Spirit:
"Make every effort to preserve the unity which has the Spirit as its
origin and peace as its binding force." Jesus created and redeemed

both the visible and invisible and therefore is concerned about both within his church.

It is the mystery of the cross that brings all this within our grasp and makes it a lived reality. Paul says, "It pleased God, . . . by means of him, to reconcile everything in his person, both on earth and in the heavens, making peace through the blood of his cross." As to the more visible fruit of the Spirit, he says, "Those who belong to Christ Jesus have crucified their flesh with its passions and desires." The mysterious hidden wisdom of Paul is nothing more or less than the cross: "I did not come proclaiming God's testimony with any particular eloquence or wisdom. . . . I would speak of nothing but Jesus Christ and him crucified."

Today's parable says that the man sold all he had and bought the field. Jesus Christ gave all he had on the cross for the church. "He emptied himself and took the form of a slave, being born in the likeness of men, . . . obediently accepting death, death on a cross!" Are we willing to do the same for the sake of Jesus and his church?

Paul says, "In my own flesh I fill up what is lacking in the sufferings of Christ for the sake of his body the church." He goes so far as to say he would go to hell so others might go to heaven! "Indeed, I could even wish to be separated from Christ for the sake of my brothers."

Yet this kind of total self-sacrifice does not go unrewarded. Jesus says of such poverty, "Sell what you have and give alms. Get purses for yourselves that do not wear out, a never-failing treasure with the Lord." Paul says to Timothy, "In this way they will lay up treasure for themselves as a firm foundation for the coming age." Are we willing to go through the cross to find such a treasure? Do we see in the visible and invisible church a treasure beyond all price? □

A Sure Foundation
Matthew 13:47-53 (17:Thursday)

Every scribe who is learned in the reign of God is like the head of a household who can bring from his storeroom both the new and the old. (v. 52)

So it is with the teachers of the church: They don't just acquire knowledge; they personally come to know the spiritual power of the reign of God. Then they teach. As Paul says, "Knowledge puffs up, love upbuilds."

Jesus says, "Do not pour new wine into old wineskins." But he also says, "The scribes and Pharisees have succeeded Moses as teachers; therefore, do everything and observe everything they tell you. But do not follow their example." He says in the Sermon on the Mount, "Do not think I have come to abolish the law and the prophets. I have come, not to abolish them, but to fulfill them." He says to his skeptics, "Search the scriptures.... They also testify on my behalf.... If you believed Moses, you would then believe me, for it was about me that he wrote."

The new covenant people, the church, also has an unfolding tradition upon which it builds: "You form a building which rises on the foundation of the apostles and prophets, with Christ Jesus himself as the capstone." The early church heard the story of Jesus, the good news, through the preaching of the apostles. The Christians "devoted themselves to the apostles' instruction." The tradition of the church must be apostolic if it is to be valid.

Out of this apostolic tradition came the Scriptures: how to interpret the old and how to compile the new. "Devote yourself to the reading of Scripture." "All Scripture is inspired of God and is useful for teaching—for reproof, correction, and training in holiness so that the man of God may be fully competent and equipped for every good work." Thus says Paul the apostle. Second Peter speaks of Paul's letters being read in the assembly as Scripture! "Paul, our beloved brother, wrote you this in the spirit of wisdom that is his, dealing with this matter as he does in all his letters. There are certain passages in them hard to understand. The ignorant and the unstable distort them (just as they do the rest of Scripture) to their own ruin."

Do we appreciate this richness of our two-thousand year history? As Paul says regarding both apostolic tradition and the Scripture it birthed, "Guard the rich deposit of faith with the help of the Holy Spirit who dwells within us."

We must build upward, but we must build solidly upon the apostolic tradition of the past if we are to become a true building or temple of the Spirit. Otherwise, what we build will surely fall. Likewise, we must not try to rebuild when some apostolic block has already been set in place. This would be a waste of precious time. Build upward, but build on the rich apostolic tradition of our past. Then will this temple of the new covenant people of God reach to the heavens and to the skies in the love and truth of God. □

Do Not Stifle the Spirit
Matthew 13:54-58 (17:Friday)

No prophet is without honor except in his native place, indeed in his own house. (v. 57)

How true this statement is! Those who live with us on a day in and day out basis might be highly regarded as men or women of God around the world, but at home they are as common as an old shoe. Sometimes this causes us to not listen to them when they speak about God.

Of Jesus they said, "Isn't this the carpenter's son? Isn't Mary known to be his mother and James, Joseph, Simon, and Judas his brothers? Aren't his sisters our neighbors? Where did he get all this?" So often this is how we treat a prophet among us. Because we think we know him, we are not open to the power of the Spirit flowing through him. With the neighbors of Jesus, we "find him altogether too much" for us. We cannot accept his mission from God.

But Paul says our local assemblies will be graced by brothers and sisters with powerful gifts of the Spirit: "To each person the manifestation of the Spirit is given for the common good. To one the Spirit gives wisdom in discourse, to another the power to express knowledge. Through the Spirit one receives faith, by the same Spirit another is given the gift of healing, and still another miraculous powers. Prophecy is given to one; to another power to distinguish one spirit from another. One receives the gift of tongues, another that of interpreting the tongues." These gifts are given to each member. Not one is exempt from receiving a gift of the Spirit. At Pentecost the Spirit fell upon "each" and "all" of them.

Yet so often we do not open ourselves to this new life in the Spirit. We impose past life-styles on those we know. We do not allow them to change. We do not allow them to be "created anew." Yet we don't allow the people we love the most to be powerfully changed by the God who is love. Because of this we see few of the gifts of God manifested in our local assemblies.

Paul says, "Anticipate each other in showing respect. Do not grow slack, but be fervent in spirit; he whom you serve is the Lord." Without this attitude the charismatic gifts will be stifled in our local communities. We must really respect the powerful work that God is doing in our brothers' and sisters' lives. Paul says, "Do not stifle the Spirit." We could also say, "Do not stifle your brother or sister."

Today's gospel says that Jesus did not work many miracles because the people lacked faith. Do you see the miracles of Jesus working in your local church or fellowship? Do you allow the extraordinary power of the Spirit to work through the common and ordinary people with whom you live and work day after day? Jesus wants to transform these relationships. He wants to make them channels of the Spirit's power and grace. Expect a miracle from Jesus, but expect it to come through the people closest to you. As Paul says, "Do not forbid" the working of the Spirit through them. □

Standing for Justice
Matthew 14:1-12 (17:Saturday)

Herod had had John arrested, put in chains, and imprisoned on account of Herodias, the wife of his brother Philip. That was because John had told him, "It is not right for you to live with her." Herod wanted to kill John. . . . He sent the order to have John beheaded in prison. (v. 3-5, 10)

Herod was morally weak. He was washed back and forth by the opinion of others. He was a compromiser. He helped the Jews deal with the Romans, but he compromised the purity of God's law in the process.

John the Baptist was no compromiser. He was strong. He rebuked Herod at the expense of his own life. Even though he lost his life, he maintained the life of purity according to God's law.

The law said, "You shall not have intercourse with your brother's wife, for that would be a disgrace to your brother." It goes on, "You shall not have intercourse with a woman and also with her daughter." It is likely that Herod was guilty of the latter also, at least in the lust of his mind if not in body.

Some people would say that John lost his head by becoming involved in the domestic and personal morality of the king. They think he would have been much wiser to be lenient with the personal sins of this government leader so as to better accomplish his greater mission among the people. I do not agree.

The basis of John's mission was personal penance: "Reform your lives! The reign of God is at hand." He did not retreat in the face of religious leaders: "When he saw that many Pharisees and Sadducees were stepping forward for his bath, he said this to them: 'You brood of vipers! Who told you to flee from the wrath to come? Give evidence that you mean to reform.'" Why should secular leaders be treated any differently?

Paul too was not afraid to speak for justice among government leaders. Offered release from the prison at Philippi, he said, "They flogged us in public without even a trial, then they threw us into jail, although we are Roman citizens! Now they want to smuggle us out in secret. Not a bit of it! Let them come into the prison and escort us out." Before Festus he said, "I have committed no crime either against the law of the Jews or against the temple or against the emperor. . . . If I am guilty, if I have committed a crime deserving death, I do not seek to escape the death penalty. But if there is nothing to the charges these men bring against me, no one has a right to hand me over to them."

Jesus too, even though meek and humble before his accusers, said in response to being hit, "If I said anything wrong produce the evidence, but if I spoke the truth why hit me?"

Are we afraid to call our government leaders to enact justice? Do we let our Christian and Catholic leaders slide by as they compromise morality in their private lives and in their legislation? Abortion, nuclear arms, the world's poor—these are all issues that demand a response in accord with God's law. Are we afraid to lose our heads as we battle to bring justice to and through the governments of our world?   □

Pray, Then Work
Matthew 14:13-21 (18:Monday)

He withdrew by boat from there to a deserted place by himself. The crowds heard of it and followed him on foot from the towns. When he disembarked and saw the vast throng, his heart was moved with pity, and he cured their sick. (v. 13-14)

This Scripture speaks of the tension between solitary prayer and apostolic action. This tension is like the string on a guitar. If there is not enough, there is no musical note. If there is too much, the string breaks. So it is with the tension between contemplation and action. If there is no tension at all, the note of our life will not clearly sound. If there is too much, we will snap, emotionally, physically, and spiritually. Yet, if the tension is just right, our life will sound like a clear musical note which, harmoniously fitted within the full chorus of the church, can make beautiful music.

The Gospels portray Jesus as a man of solitude: "He often retired to deserted places and prayed," says Luke. Yet this prayer was integrated with action: "He went out to the mountain to pray, spending the night in communion with God" before he chose the twelve apostles and preached the great sermon to many of his disciples. He was transfigured on Mount Tabor during a similar sojourn in prayer with James, Peter, and John. He came down from this mountain to solve the apostles' inability to cast out a demon. Before the trial and crucifixion Jesus spent another such night in communion with God, again with the closest of his apostles, Peter, James, and John. Many more examples could be shown if space allowed.

What does this say? First, there seems to be an alternation between Jesus' prayer and his work. He prays, and prays long, then he goes out to minister. Second, he seems to take along a few companions even during these night vigils. He does not take all of the twelve; he only takes the three who are closest to him. Thus, even in contemplative prayer, Jesus is united with his closest apostles.

Francis of Assisi followed a similar pattern. Almost all the great and memorable moments and miracles of his life occurred at a hermitage. And the hermitage itself was not reclusive but was a place where three or four brothers prayed together in the solitude of a hermit's cell and in the unity of brothers in a chapel. This is why Francis's works for Jesus were so great! They were patterned on the life of Jesus, and they flowed forth from prayerful union with Jesus.

And what about us? Is our life rooted in prayer? Some will undoubtedly say, "My work is my prayer." But in light of the example of Christ, this is not enough. We need actual times of prayer and solitude. We must provide an environment conducive to quiet communion with Christ. This means an intentional choice. This means preferring prayer over work at specific times in our life. Only then will our work really feed the hungry multitudes. □

Wasting Time with Jesus
Matthew 14:22-36 (18:Tuesday)

When he had sent them away, he went up on the mountain by himself to pray, remaining there as evening drew on. Meanwhile the boat, already several hundred yards out from shore, was being tossed about in the waves raised by strong head winds. At about three in the morning, he came walking toward them on the lake. (v. 23-25)

Here Jesus goes back into solitude. He tried before, in yesterday's gospel, but was interrupted by the crowds. Today he tries again. Even Jesus needed to persist in finding solitude for prayer. Otherwise he could not properly commune with the Father and be revitalized by the Spirit. After all, didn't he himself teach us, "Whenever you pray, go to your room, close your door, and pray to your Father in private"? In today's gospel he tries again to fulfill his own teaching.

But notice that without his presence the boat is tossed by the waves. When Jesus was with them he would calm the waves. When he was absent the waves engulfed them again. Without Jesus progress was difficult.

Isn't this how it is when we try to get away to pray? Just when we feel we absolutely must get away, some crisis in our community or church comes up. We might feel on the edge of a nervous breakdown, but something always comes up to prevent us from our much-needed retreat with Jesus. Be at peace, Jesus had the same problem, yet he took the time to pray.

Through this a great miracle occurred. Jesus broke away from his "community" to pray in solitude. Yet he was still able to help them when a real crisis occurred. He relied on miraculous powers that come from communion with God in solitary prayer! After prayer, Jesus came to them across the waters. He took time to pray, so a miracle occurred. He met his own spiritual needs through prayer, then he was able to meet the needs of his community through a miracle. Without solitary prayer none of these needs would have been met by God.

Do we take the time to break away? There will always be a "good" reason not to pray. The work will always be there. It takes faith to break away from our work or ministry to "waste time" with Jesus. Yet if we do, then our work will be filled with the miraculous power of the Spirit of God. □

Jesus Looks to the Heart
Matthew 15:21-28 (18:Wednesday)

"My mission is only to the lost sheep of the house of Israel". .... "Please, Lord," she insisted, "even the dogs eat the leavings that fall from their masters' tables." Jesus then said in reply, "Woman, you have great faith! Your wish will come to pass." (v. 24, 27-28)

How do we respond to those outside of our church? Do we passively recognize their salvation but treat them like outsiders? Jesus' primary mission was to the house of Israel, but he made exceptions in the cases of faithful outsiders.

Jesus spoke to the woman at the well in Samaria, even though it was considered scandalous to speak to such "heretics." He also told the parable of the Good Samaritan, in which the Samaritan's charity places him above the "orthodox" priest and scribe. Jesus said of the Roman centurion, "Never have I found such faith in all of Israel," even though the Romans were looked upon as unjust military oppressors by the Jews. In today's gospel he offers healing and salvation to a Canaanite woman, even though the Canaanites and the Jews were longtime enemies. Jesus had a definite understanding of his mission in Israel, but he also knew he was to be a "light to the nations."

Today's gospel, along with these other examples, brings out the difference between orthodoxy, or right belief, and right practice. While Jesus and the apostles definitely emphasize the need for orthodoxy within the church, Jesus especially sees the good intentions behind the actions of those who might hold theologically erroneous views—and he "counts it to them as righteousness."

Today's church sometimes suffers from an inconsistency between these two concepts. Sometimes those who hold and fight for orthodoxy are the very ones who act least righteously. They might hold all the right doctrines, but they are not really Christlike in their actions toward other people. This nullifies the value of their orthodoxy. In fact, the Gospels indicate that Jesus will judge a person's soul more on the intentions behind their actions than on their doctrinal orthodoxy! Ideally, orthodoxy yields right practice, but this is not always the case.

It is like the difference between a fine restaurant and a fast-food place. The restaurant might have better food, but if there is no one to wait tables the people will go down the street to the fast-food place. The food might not be as good, but at least they get served!

So in the traditional church, how can we fault those who go to the "fast-food" churches when we are not properly waiting tables? We might be more orthodox, but if our actions do not match our orthodoxy, it will do us and them no good.

How do we judge a person's faith? Do we discern only according to doctrine, or do we look to their intent? Jesus seems to look past doctrine to the intent behind a person's action of faith. Can we who really follow Jesus do anything but the same? □

The Life of the Church
Matthew 16:13-23 (18:Thursday)

"Who do you say that I am?" "You are the Messiah," Simon Peter answered, "the Son of the living God!" Jesus replied, "Blest are you, Simon son of John! No mere man has revealed this to you, but my heavenly Father. I for my part declare to you, you are 'Rock,' and on this rock I will build my church." (v. 15-18)

Today's gospel is rich with lessons. They cover both the objective and subjective aspects of our faith. They also cover that which applies to our private and corporate relationship with God, as individuals and as church.

Of course, much has been made of this Scripture by Catholics as to the role of Peter and his papal successors in the leadership of the church. There are arguments concerning the meaning of Jesus' words, "You are 'Rock,' and upon this rock I will build my church." Some say that while *Rock* refers to Peter, the "rock" upon which the church would be built is Jesus. This seems a rather contrived interpretation, especially in light of the other words of

Jesus concerning Peter and the understanding of the early church fathers. [Yet Jesus, the chief shepherd, said specifically to Peter after the resurrection, "Feed my sheep."] This Scripture, in light of early church teaching, led to the Catholic understanding of the primacy of Peter, of his taking the visible place of Jesus among the apostles after the Ascension. After all, every tribe has a council and a chief. Likewise, Catholics have a college of bishops and a presiding bishop over them. What better authority to build on concerning who that leader should be than that of Jesus himself and his words in Scripture.

But this is not to neglect the primary role of Christ as head of the church. Here Protestant and Catholic agree. As Paul says, "It is he who is head of the body, the church; he who is the beginning, the firstborn of the dead, so that primacy may be his in everything." And he says to the Ephesians, "You form a building which rises on the foundation of the apostles and prophets, with Christ Jesus himself as the capstone." He continues, "Through him the whole structure is fitted together and takes shape as a holy temple in the Lord; in him you are being built into this temple, to become a dwelling place for God in the Spirit."

It is here that we pass from the corporate and objective understanding of the Christian faith to the personal experience of Christ himself. The Spirit is given not only to the church in common but to each individual. As the Acts of the Apostles says, "Tongues as of fire appeared, which parted and came to rest on each of them. All were filled with the Holy Spirit." Or conversely, as Paul says to the Romans, "If anyone does not have the Spirit of Christ, he does not belong to Christ."

This aspect of faith is highly mystical. It is a personal experience, a love relationship. In today's gospel Peter had personally and mystically come to the knowledge that Jesus is the Christ, the Messiah. "No mere man has revealed this to you, but my heavenly Father." As Paul says to the Corinthians, "No one knows what lies at the depths of God but the Spirit of God. . . . What we utter is God's wisdom; a mysterious, a hidden wisdom. Yet God has revealed this wisdom to us through the Spirit." And conversely, "the natural man does not accept what is taught by the Spirit of God."

This personal experience of Christ is the ultimate goal of the teaching of the whole Christian church. Jesus says to those rejected at the last judgment, "I never knew you." He says in Revelation, "Here I stand, knocking at the door. If anyone hears me calling and opens the door, I will enter his house and have supper with him and he with me."

Have we opened the door of our personal house to Jesus? Do we know Jesus personally, or is he just a matter of church doctrine and liturgical celebration? Today we are called to personally answer the question, "Who do you say that I am?" Only then will we really understand the life of the church. □

The Great Risk
Matthew 16:24-28 (18:Friday)

If a man wishes to come after me, he must deny his very self, take up his cross, and begin to follow in my footsteps. Whoever would save his life will lose it, but whoever loses his life for my sake will find it. (v. 24-25)

This morning I am struck by the ways Jesus practiced what he preached. We assume that Jesus was trained as a carpenter, yet we never hear of him using this skill at all during his ministry. Jesus himself had to break with his past and venture forth into the desert, there to be trained for his new way of life in ministry.

Paul says, "The things I used to consider gain I have now reappraised as loss in light of Christ. For his sake I have forfeited everything; I have accounted all else rubbish so Christ may be my wealth." Paul was once a Pharisee, an up-and-coming man in the religious world of the Jews. He gave it all up. He gained only the life of this new Messiah, the life of this Jesus of Nazareth. Paul was going to be "really something," yet he risked becoming nothing for Christ. His name will be remembered throughout all of human history, only because he was first willing to crucify all he was, or ever hoped to be, with Jesus Christ. As he himself said, "May I never boast of anything but the cross of our Lord Jesus Christ."

How many times I am unwilling to do this! I would much rather "baptize" my natural talents and use them for the Lord. While there is nothing wrong with this in itself, it usually requires much less of an actual death to the past than the radical example of Jesus. It often leads to mediocrity in the name of moderation.

A total and complete break with the past leads us to the highways and byways with Jesus to live the radical life of the gospel that he proclaimed. It ushers us into a literal and graphic experience of the first apostles and disciples, who walked with Jesus in Galilee and Judea, trusting totally in the providence of God to provide for their needs. □

Purity and Power
Matthew 17:14-20 [21] (18:Saturday)

"Why could we not expel it?" "Because you have so little trust," he told them. . . . "This kind does not leave but by prayer and fasting." (v. 19-20, 21)

Why is it we see so few miracles in our lives? Is it because we do not try to work them? Or is it because we secretly do not believe that God will really work healings and miracles through the likes of us? As Jesus says, if we have no inner doubts but believe that what we say will happen, it shall be done for us.

The disciples tried to work a miracle for the possessed boy and his father, but they could not. They had been empowered by Jesus to do this kind of miracle. Jesus had said, "Cure the sick, raise the dead, heal the leprous, expel demons." They had even enjoyed success in doing this in Jesus' name: "Master, even the demons are subject to us in your name." Yet in today's gospel we find them unable to cast out a devil. The boy's father says to Jesus, "I have brought him to your disciples but they could not cure him."

We know that even those who did not directly associate with Jesus and the apostles were able to use Jesus' name successfully. John once said to Jesus, "Master, we saw a man using your name to expel demons, and we tried to stop him because he was not of our company." Jesus responded, "Do not stop him, for any man who is not against you is on your side."

The Jewish exorcists in Ephesus did not always meet with such a favorable response. While some itinerant exorcists seemed to be successful in casting out demons in Jesus' name, others received this response from the demons: "Jesus I recognize, Paul I know, but who are you?" The account continues, "Then the man with the evil spirit sprang at them and overpowered them all. He dealt with them so violently that they fled from his house naked and bruised." Apparently neither the power of demons nor the power of Jesus' name is to be taken lightly. As the account ends, "When this became known to the Jews and Greeks living in Ephesus, fear fell upon all, and the name of the Lord Jesus came to be held in great reverence."

Jesus says of some demons, "This kind does not leave but by prayer and fasting." This means that a person's life must coincide with the miracle he or she seeks to work in Jesus' name. One cannot presume to work a miracle when living in sin or away from Christ. Superficial belief is not enough. Even the devils believe! One's faith must be deep enough to transform one's whole life. As James says, "Do you believe that God is one? You are quite right. The demons believe that and shudder. . . . Be assured, then, that faith without works is dead." As he says of those who ask without faith, "A man of this sort . . . must not expect to receive anything from the Lord."

If you fast and pray, your life will be changed. Then your faith will deepen and the devils will be cast out. As Paul says, "I plead with you then, as a prisoner for the Lord, to live a life worthy of the calling you have received."

Even success in such miracles is no guarantee of holiness. Jesus says that some who are rejected at the judgment will cry out, "Lord, Lord, have we not prophesied in your name? Have we not exorcised demons by its power?" He said to the disciples, "Do not rejoice so much in the fact that the devils are subject to you as that your names are inscribed in heaven."

Do we meet with success when operating in the charismatic gifts of miracles, healing, and deliverance? If we do not, perhaps our life is not yet worthy of our call. Even if we do meet with great success in ministering the gifts of the Spirit, perhaps our lives are not yet really holy. Perhaps this is really the strongest of all devils that can be cast out only by fasting and prayer. ☐

Submissive but Fearless
Matthew 17:22-27 (19:Monday)

But for fear of disedifying them go to the lake, throw in a line and take out the first fish you catch. Open its mouth and you will discover there a coin worth twice the temple tax. Take it and give it to them for you and me. (v. 27)

Today we hear much talk about civil disobedience and the refusal to pay civil taxes. Today's gospel deals with a religious rather than a civil tax, but many of the principles are the same.

Jesus himself disagrees with the concept of the temple tax, based on the ethics of the secular world. "Do the kings of the world take tax or toll from their sons or from foreigners?" he asks Peter. When Peter replies, "From foreigners," Jesus observes, "Then their sons are exempt." Jesus disagrees with the concept of the temple tax, yet he pays it anyway. He actually works a miracle to do so!

How contrary this is to the movements in the church today that advocate civil disobedience and religious dissent! Jesus teaches nonresistance and love. We look in vain to support our religious dissent with the example of a Christ who said, "The scribes and Pharisees have succeeded Moses as teachers; therefore, do everything and observe everything they tell you," even though he adds, "But do not follow their example."

As we shall see later in Matthew's Gospel, Jesus also advocated payment of civil taxes, even to an unjust government that oppresses its people. The Roman Empire had conquered the Jews and occupied their land. Sure, the Romans brought many of the advancements of their civilization to the more primitive Jewish kingdom, but they still oppressed them. Many if not most of the religious sects of Jesus' day worked to eventually remove the Romans from their land. It seemed evident to all that this effort was acceptable and just. Yet when they asked Jesus, "Is it lawful to pay tax to the emperor or not?" Jesus responded, "Give to Caesar what is Caesar's, but give to God what is God's." We do not find in the life of Jesus Christ any strong support for civil disobedience.

St. Paul too says, "Let everyone obey the authorities that are over him, for there is no authority except from God. The man who opposes authority rebels against the ordinance of God. . . . You pay taxes for the same reason. . . . Pay each one his due: taxes to whom taxes are due; toll to whom toll is due." And Peter says, "Because of the Lord, be obedient to every human institution, whether to the emperor as sovereign or to the governor he commissions. Such obedience is the will of God."

On the other hand, Jesus was not afraid to speak the truth. He overturned the moneychangers' tables, saying, "Scripture has it, 'My house shall be called a house of prayer,' but you are turning it into a den of thieves." Peter was not afraid to say to the Sanhedrin, "Better for us to obey God than men!" And Paul was not afraid to invoke his civil rights as a Roman citizen when he said, "Is it legal to flog a Roman citizen without a trial?" We too are called to speak boldly to both religious and civil authorities, but always in submitted humility and selfless love. Only on rare occasions may we actually dissent.

Do we approach our civil or religious dissent with proper humility? Are we so humble that we would even attempt to work a miracle in order to keep the peace? Civil disobedience and theological dissent are not games to be played by those who enjoy controversy. At best, they are cautiously entered into by those who only seek unity and peace. Even then, we must respect and try to submit to those who are in religious and civil authority. Any other way cannot validly be called Christian, for it is not "like Christ." ☐

The Humility to Receive
Matthew 18:1-5, 10, 12-14 (19:Tuesday)

I assure you, unless you change and become like little children, you will not enter into the kingdom of God. . . . Whoever welcomes one such child for my sake welcomes me. . . . It is no part of your heavenly Father's plan that a single one of these little ones shall ever come to grief. (v. 3, 5, 14)

Today's gospel speaks of both becoming childlike and welcoming other children, of becoming humble before God and of becoming humble before others. In the first instance God helps us; in the second we help others. Both work together in accomplishing God's plan of salvation.

How many of us approach the spiritual gifts with a subtle spiritual pride? Oh, yes, some of us take credit for our gifts, but this is an obvious spiritual pride. I am talking about something more subtle, something that even appears to be humble! I refer to the person who says, "The charismatic gifts are good, but I am not worthy of such gifts." Many times, instead of this reflecting genuine humility, it only indicates a person's fear of entering into something new from God. Such a one values his or her "safety" more than he or she trusts God's goodness. This is spiritual pride.

Paul says, "Set your hearts on spiritual gifts." He even says, "Set your hearts on the greater gifts." Concerning the controversial gift of tongues he says, "I should like it if all of you spoke in tongues," and, "Thank God, I speak in tongues more than any of you." Think of it: The great saint of the church, Paul the apostle, was a Pentecostal! He was humble enough to accept whatever gift God wanted to give him.

If a parent had a wonderful gift to give a child and the child did not show any interest in the gift at all, would the child be thought humble? No! The child would be thought arrogant and spoiled. At best the child would be just downright stupid!

So it is with spiritual gifts. The Father wants to give each of us wonderful gifts, as we are legitimate children of mother church. How can we be so stupid and proud as to turn away from them? They are for our good and the good of the church. As Paul says, "To each person the manifestation of the Spirit is given for the common good." To stifle the Spirit is an act against God's goodness. Again, "Do not stifle the Spirit. Do not despise prophecies," and, "Do not forbid those who speak in tongues, but make sure that everything is done properly and in order."

Once we approach the gifts of God with such humility and openness, we will find that, in fact, all of us will not receive the same gifts. Paul says, "Are all apostles? Are all prophets? Are all teachers? Do all work miracles or have the gift of healing? Do all speak in tongues?" The obvious answer is no. The only gift we must all have is the gift of love.

The charismatic gifts of the Spirit are nothing without the love that causes us to be humble before our brothers and sisters. Paul says clearly, "If I speak with human tongues and angelic as well, but do not have love, I am a noisy gong, a clanging cymbal. . . . Love does not put on airs, it is not snobbish." Of this humility he says elsewhere, "Let all parties think humbly of others as superior to themselves." And to the Romans, "Anticipate each other in showing respect. Put away ambitious thoughts and associate with those who are lowly. Do not be wise in your own estimation. Extend a kind welcome to those who are weak in faith."

Do we really seek the gifts of the Holy Spirit in our life? Are we humble enough to ask God for the gifts which we so desperately need? Jesus says, "If you, with all your sins, know how to give good things to your children, how much more will the heavenly Father give the Holy Spirit to those who ask him." Today let us be like children before God. Let us ask for the Spirit. Then we will also be humble and kind before one another. □

Strength in Numbers
Matthew 18:15-20 (19:Wednesday)

If he ignores even the church, then treat him as you would a Gentile or a tax collector. . . . Where two or three are gathered in my name, there am I in their midst. (v. 17, 20)

Today's gospel speaks of the power of the church, the strength of the Spirit working through the many rather than the one. It speaks of a wisdom and a sureness that is found in the discernment of the whole church, rather than in the private judgment of only one soul.

We know this is true regarding the interpretation of Scripture. Peter says in his second letter, "There is no prophecy contained in Scripture which is a personal interpretation." We know that the Spirit has been given to all believers, to "guide you to all truth," and consequently, as John says, "This means you have no need for anyone to teach you." Yet part of that anointing of the Spirit was for the apostles to "make disciples of all the nations" and "teach them to carry out everything I have commanded you." As Paul says, "God has set up in the church first apostles, second prophets, third teachers." This is a work of the Spirit, but it involves the official teaching authority of the church.

It was with this Spirit that the apostles were given the power of the keys. This is the power of judgment in leadership to even discern to some degree the sincerity of a person's faith and to judge how to strengthen it through both love and discipline. Jesus said specifically to his apostles, "Receive the Holy Spirit. If you forgive men's sins, they are forgiven them; if you hold them bound, they are held bound."

This is what today's gospel describes when it speaks of the church treating one as a Gentile or tax collector. Paul says to the Corinthians regarding the incestuous brother, "I wrote you in my letter not to associate with immoral persons. I was not speaking of association with immoral people in this world. To avoid them, you would have to leave the world! What I really wrote about was your not associating with anyone who bears the title 'brother' if he is immoral." Paul then uses his apostolic authority: "I hand him over to Satan for the destruction of his flesh, so that his spirit may be saved on the day of the Lord." Notice this judgment is not for the man's destruction but for his salvation. Paul knew he had this authority, and he used it for the good of the erring brother and for the good of the church.

More important is the strength found in communal spiritual discernment within the church. Paul sought the discernment of the other apostles rather than trusting in his own private experience: "I laid out for their scrutiny the gospel I present to the Gentiles—to make sure the course I was pursuing, or had pursued, was not useless." As Sirach says, "Frequent the company of elders." Proverbs says, "In the counsel of many there is wisdom." It was as a community that the apostles chose Mathias to replace Judas (see Acts 1:15-26). It was as a community that the apostles dealt with practical problems in the church, such as the need for assistants (Acts 6:1-7) and the problems of Gentile converts (Acts 15:1-35).

The same holds true for the strength and power of communal prayer. As today's gospel says, "If two or three of you join your voices on earth to pray for anything whatever, it shall be granted you by my Father in heaven." It was when the disciples were gathered together that the power of the Spirit fell: "When the day of Pentecost came it found them gathered in one place." After that came "tongues as of fire" and "bold proclamations" in the Spirit. So it was that even in the early church "they were engaged in the liturgy of the Lord and were fasting." There is great power in the united liturgical prayer of the church.

Do we keep our religion private? Sure, Jesus says, "Whenever you pray, go to your room, close your door, and pray to your Father in private." But he also speaks in today's gospel about the corporate authority and power of the church. The experience of the early church shows a balance between the private and the public dimensions of our faith. It shows a power of the Holy Spirit manifested on both levels. Do we limit the work of the Spirit primarily to one or the other? The private without the public is proud, and the public without the private will never reach full spiritual depth. □

The Facts about Forgiveness
Matthew 18:21-19:1 (19:Thursday)

"Lord, when my brother wrongs me, how often must I forgive him? Seven times?" "No," Jesus replied, "not seven times; I say, seventy times seven times." (v. 21-22)

So often we are like Peter. We are willing to forgive our brother or sister up to a point, but when they repeatedly make the same mistake, we draw the line and cut them off. We must understand that the line we draw, the cutoff point, is usually our line, not God's.

In yesterday's gospel we spoke of a valid judgment in the church by the apostles. But this judgment was only if the brother "does not listen" to the church. Jesus says in Luke's Gospel, "If your brother does wrong, correct him; if he repents, forgive him. If he sins against you seven times a day, and seven times a day turns back to you saying, 'I am sorry,' forgive him." Jesus' use of the number seven implies infinity. There is no cutoff point for forgiveness within the church. Forgiveness is always available for those who repent, no matter how great their sin.

Notice, however, that repentance precedes forgiveness. Jesus says, "In [the Messiah's] name, penance for the remission of sins is to be preached to all the nations." God's forgiveness is like a constant and gentle rain upon all peoples of the earth. However, it takes a bucket to catch the rain; that bucket is repentance. Without our own personal repentance, or change, God's forgiveness does not become effective in our life.

This is why John the Baptist told the crowds who came to him, "Give some evidence that you mean to reform." Both John the Baptist and Jesus Christ taught, "Reform your lives. The kingdom of heaven is at hand." Some visible change in a person's life was expected as evidence of a change of heart.

Paul might rightly emphasize interior faith, saying, "Salvation is yours by faith. This is not your own doing, it is God's gift; neither is it a reward for anything you have accomplished." To the Galatians he says, "A man is not justified by legal observance but by faith in Jesus Christ." James also says, "You must perceive that a person is justified by his works and not by faith alone. . . . Faith without works is dead as a body without breath." Faith is a gift from God! But if faith is real it brings forth repentance, and if repentance is real it is reflected in our works.

It was this balance between forgiveness and repentance, between faith and works, that was seen in Paul's dealings with the incestuous man in Corinth. Yesterday we saw how Paul was not afraid to exclude this man from the community of believers. In his second letter he says, "The punishment already inflicted by the majority on such a one is enough; you should now relent and support him so that he may not be crushed by too great a weight of sorrow." Later he says, "If I saddened you by my letter I have no regrets. . . . Indeed, sorrow for God's sake produces a repentance without regrets, leading to salvation, whereas worldly sorrow brings death." Thus, even Paul's just judgment gave way to forgiveness and support of the weaker brother.

The early church enrolled people into the class of "penitents" for a period of time if they committed grave public sin. A publicly known murderer, adulterer, or whatever would be a penitent for a period of time to test the sincerity of his professed repentance. During this time such persons could not receive Communion, even though they were still considered brothers and sisters in Christ. If their conversion was sincere, they would humbly and patiently wait a time before receiving Communion, grateful for receiving God's forgiveness at all! After this testing time the community would receive them back into full fellowship at the table of the Lord.

The bottom line is in the "golden rule" of Christianity, "Love your neighbor as yourself." Paul says, "Forgive as the Lord has forgiven you." How can we withhold forgiveness from others when God has been so merciful to us?

As the parable of today's gospel says to the merciless official, "You worthless wretch! I cancelled your entire debt when you pleaded with me. Should you not have dealt mercifully with your fellow servant, as I dealt with you?" Then Jesus speaks of God's judgment on those who will not forgive, saying, "My heavenly Father will treat you in exactly the same way unless each of you forgives his brother from his heart."   □

Two High Callings
Matthew 19:3-12 (19:Friday)

Whoever divorces his wife (lewd conduct is a separate case) and marries another commits adultery, and the man who marries a divorced woman commits adultery. . . . Not everyone can accept this teaching, only those to whom it is given to do so. . . . Some there are who have freely renounced sex for the sake of God's reign. Let him accept this teaching who can. (v. 9, 11, 12)

Today Jesus teaches on two vocational calls, marriage and celibacy. Jesus' teaching is especially helpful as we face an outbreak of promiscuous sexual behavior in our Western civilization, which manifests itself in a rash of divorces among those called to marriage and in a declining number of people willing to "renounce sex for the sake of God's reign" in celibacy.

Paul speaks clearly about promiscuous sexual behavior: "As for lewd conduct or promiscuousness or lust of any sort, let them not even be mentioned among you; your holiness forbids this. . . . Make no mistake about this: No fornicator, no unclean or lustful person—in effect an idolater—has any inheritance in the kingdom of Christ and of God. Let no one deceive you with worthless arguments."

There are, of course, many Scriptures which speak about sexual immorality. The church bases its authoritative teaching on all of these. In the end, genital expressions of sexuality between a husband and wife for the sake of personal love union and procreation are seen as God's perfect plan. This is why the church has always taught that masturbation, homosexuality, and pre-marital and extramarital sex are sinful. All of these eventually lead to sexuality for selfish reasons, which leads to lust, which finally leads to spiritual and even physical death. If any one aspect of the church's teaching about sexuality is missing, sexuality degenerates and brings forth pastoral and cultural death. History has proven this many times.

Paul also restates Jesus' teaching on divorce; "A wife must not separate from her husband. Similarly, a husband must not separate from his wife." It is assumed that Christian marriages simply will not end in divorce, for Christians simply will not be involved in sexual immorality.

But Paul does make exception when one partner of the marriage is not Christian: "If the unbeliever wishes to separate, however, let him do so. The believing husband or wife is not bound in such cases." This does not rule out the need for these "mixed" marriages to stay together whenever possible: "If any brother has a wife who is an unbeliever but is willing to live with him, he must not divorce her. And if any woman has a husband who is an unbeliever but is willing to live with her, she must not divorce him. The unbelieving husband is consecrated by his believing wife; the unbelieving wife is consecrated by her believing husband."

This final point is definitely a development of apostolic tradition, Paul says, "Although I know of nothing the Lord has said, I say ..." But perhaps even this is based on the Lord's words, "lewd conduct is a separate case," assuming that only a non-Christian would leave his or her spouse for another partner. Again, for Christians, lewd conduct was not even a possibility!

As to celibacy Paul says, "A man is better off having no relations with a woman. To those not married and to widows, I have this to say: It would be well if they remain as they are, even as I do myself." This is for practical reasons. He says, "The unmarried man is busy with the Lord's affairs, but the married man is busy with the world's demands and occupied with pleasing his wife." As Jesus says, celibacy is practiced "for the sake of God's reign." But Jesus' reasons are also mystical and eschatological: "When people rise from the dead, they neither marry nor are given in marriage, but live like angels in heaven."

As to marriage Paul continues, "But if they cannot exercise self-control, they should marry. If anyone thinks he is behaving dishonorably toward his virgin . . . he commits no sin if there is a marriage. To sum up: the man who marries his virgin acts fittingly; the one who does not will do better."

This led theologians of later centuries to an erroneous conclusion: that celibacy was superior because the sexual act of marriage was sinful and was only permitted out of the necessity of procreation in God's plan. But Paul says clearly and to the contrary, "To avoid immorality, every man should have his own wife and every woman her husband. Do not deprive one another, unless perhaps by mutual consent for a time, to devote yourselves to prayer. Then return to one another, that Satan may not tempt you through your lack of self-control." Thus, the same Paul who says that celibacy is better than marriage also says that sex in marriage is good precisely because it helps people avoid immorality, not simply because it results in procreation. Celibacy is only considered better because of its mystical symbolism of our eternal state in heaven and its practical ramifications here on earth, not because sex in itself is sinful.

In the end both celibacy and marriage are gifts from God. As Paul says, "Still, each one has his own gift from God, one this and another that." As Jesus says today, "Not everyone can accept this teaching, only those to whom it is given to do so."

Can we accept God's gift regarding our own sexuality? If we are called to celibacy, we are to be a sign of chastity in the midst of a promiscuous world. If we are called to Christian marriage, we are to be a sign of faithfulness in a world where divorce and sexual immorality are acceptable and common. Either call is clearly countercultural. Both stand in clear opposition to the sexual promiscuity of our Western world. Do you have the courage and the fortitude to stand firm in a faith that calls you to a higher sexuality than that offered by our modern world? If not, perhaps you should reconsider whether you should really call yourself a Christian. ☐

Mature Children
Matthew 19:13-15 (19:Saturday)

Let the children come to me. Do not hinder them. The kingdom of God belongs to such as these. (v. 14)

We must become like children to enter into the kingdom of God. But what is a child like? Children are certainly not perfect or sinless. Anyone who has watched even the smallest of children play together has no doubt noticed the selfish impulses that often motivate them. Granted, this is sometimes but an immature instinct for self-survival. But sometimes it is blatant self-centeredness; it is a sin! As Paul said, "All have sinned and fallen short of the glory of God." This includes children. An evangelist once said, if you are not convinced that even children are sinners, put two of them in one room with one chocolate bar, then you will find out how charitable they are!

But one quality of children we can emulate is their trust. Children have to be trusting. They depend on their parents and other grown-ups for their survival—and they know it! Left to itself at birth, a child would die. It must have its mother's milk or the assistance of doctors and nurses if it is to survive. Even an abused child will trust his or her parents for quite a while before growing embittered.

This trust is a virtue. As Paul says of the charismatic gift of love, "There is no limit to love's forbearance, to its trust, its hope, its power to endure." Children seem to possess these essential traits of love. In this they are very close to God, for as John tells us, "God is love."

This childlike attitude is a part of one who is "born again." In John's Gospel, Nicodemus asks, "How can a man be born again once he is old? Can he return to his mother's womb and be born over again?" Jesus replies, "I solemnly assure you, no one can enter into God's kingdom without being begotten of water and Spirit." Paul elaborates on this theme: "All who are led by the Spirit of God are called sons of God. . . . You did not receive a spirit of slavery leading you back into fear, but a spirit of adoption through which we cry out, 'Abba!' (that is, 'Father'). The Spirit himself gives witness with our spirit that we are children of God."

But Paul does not want us to be childish in our childlikeness. Regarding the charismatic gifts he says, "Brothers, do not be childish in your outlook. Be like children as far as evil is concerned, but in mind be mature." He says to the Ephesians, "Live as children of light. Light produces every kind of goodness and judgment and truth. Be correct in your judgment of what pleases the Lord. . . . Keep careful watch over your conduct. Do not act like fools, but like thoughtful men." This hardly sounds like the conduct of immature children. As the letter to the Hebrews encourages, "Let us, then, go beyond the initial teaching about Christ and advance to maturity."

Paul even speaks of the whole church maturing together as we advance through the years and the ages: "It is he who gave us apostles, prophets, evangelists, pastors, and teachers in roles of service for the faithful to build up the body of Christ, till we become one in faith and in knowledge of God's Son, and form that perfect man who is Christ come to full stature." As we mature as a church, the body of Christ, Jesus is actually realized and matured in us! This is a great mystery.

Do we seek a maturity that is based on childlike trust in God? Or do we seek a worldly wisdom that is, in essence, childish? Furthermore, in our exercise of the charismatic gifts, do we confuse childlikeness with childishness? Paul says, "You know that when you were pagans you were led astray as impulse drove you." The wind of the Spirit involves more than just impulse; it involves mature discernment. As Paul says, "Do not stifle the Spirit. Do not despise prophecies. Test everything, retain what is good." We are to have a balance between childlike openness to God's gifts and mature discernment of the Spirit. □

All-out for Christ
Matthew 19:16-22 (20:Monday)

If you seek perfection, go, sell your possessions, and give to the poor. You will then have treasure in heaven. Afterword; come back and follow me. (v. 21)

So many theologians have tried to rationalize these words of Christ! "It is only because Jesus knew the rich man was too attached to his possessions that he was asked to actually give them to the poor," they say. They have tried to dull the sharpness of his words, for his words threaten to cut away at our own possessions. But a sharp knife can cut to heal, while a dull knife only maims. Our rationalistic theologies have wounded the whole church for many centuries. Let us now unsheathe and sharpen the knife of healing, the sword of God's word, so that the cancer of materialism in our modern world can be healed by heeding these simple words of Christ.

Jesus says clearly, "None of you can be my disciple if he does not renounce all his possessions," and, "The unbelievers of this world are always running after these things. Seek out instead his kingship over you, and the rest will follow in turn. Do not live in fear, little flock. It has pleased your Father to give you the kingdom. Sell what you have and give alms. Get purses for yourselves that do not wear out, a never-failing treasure with the Lord which no thief comes near nor any moth destroys. Wherever your treasure lies, there your heart will be."

True, Jesus also says, "If you cannot be trusted with elusive wealth, who will trust you with lasting?" Yet he goes on to point out, "You cannot give yourself to God and money." These words are simple. These words are sharp and clear!

In accordance with Jesus' words, the early church in Jerusalem "shared all things in common; they would sell their property and goods, dividing everything on the basis of each one's need." Perhaps it was partly because of this extraordinary example of love that "day by day the Lord added to their number those who were being saved."

Throughout the other churches a similar approach to possessions was practiced, even though common ownership was not always evident. Paul says, "Buyers should conduct themselves as though they owned nothing, and those who make use of the world as though they were not using it." Yet he warns moderation: "The relief of others ought not to impoverish you; there should be a certain equality. Your plenty at the present time should supply their need so that their surplus may one day supply your need, with equality as the result." Paul admits this is a permissive teaching when he says that Jesus, our greatest example, "for your sake made himself poor though he was rich, so that you might become rich by his poverty." Little equality here. All was for others, for you and me.

Do we even meet this minimum approach to materialism in today's church? Is there any equality between our rich and our poor? Is there equality in our local parish? Is there equality between our suburban and our inner-city communities? Finally, is there equality between the church of the first and the third world? I am afraid the answer on all counts is a rather sad and disgraceful no. We in the modern church do not even meet the minimum standard of a New Testament approach to materialism.

In today's gospel the rich young ruler "went away sad, for his possessions were many." In the face of the Lord's call to us today, will we do the same? □

No Pain, No Gain
Matthew 19:23-30 (20:Tuesday)

Everyone who has given up home, brothers or sisters, father or mother, wife or children or property for my sake will receive many times as much and inherit everlasting life. (v. 29)

Today's Scripture calls us to great sacrifice. It also promises even greater reward. Two mistakes are usually made in interpreting this Scripture. One is that people want the reward without the sacrifice. The other is that people call for the sacrifice without remembering the reward.

The reward is twofold. Jesus says we "will receive many times as much *and* inherit everlasting life." In Mark's Gospel he says we "will receive in this present age a hundred times as many—and in the age to come, everlasting life."

This is seen quite practically in the early church. At Jerusalem "the community of believers were of one heart and mind. None of them ever claimed anything as his own; rather everything was held in common. Nor was there anyone needy among them, for all who owned property or houses sold them and donated the proceeds." In giving up all they gained more—more material security, more numbers in family. They gave up the little they had and gained at least "a hundred times as many."

This reward is also part of the paradox of gospel poverty. Paul says, "If we have food and clothing we have all that we need." When Jesus sent the apostles out on mission he said, "Provide yourselves with neither gold nor silver nor copper in your belts; no traveling bag, no change of shirt, no sandals, no walking staff." He said later, "When I sent you on mission without purse or traveling bag or sandals, were you in need of anything?" They replied, "Not a thing." The less you have, the less you have to pay for and maintain; therefore, the freer you are in the world.

As is said of the first Franciscans, "Because they had nothing, loved nothing, they feared in no way to lose anything. They were, therefore, everywhere secure, kept in no suspense by fears, distracted by no care, nor were they in anxiety." Because they owned nothing, all the world was theirs!

Also, gospel poverty makes us peaceful, whereas worldly poverty without Christ brings war. As Francis once said, "If we had possessions we should also be forced to have arms to protect them, since possessions are the cause for disputes and strife." The less you have, the less you have to defend!

This poverty also frees us from the fear of persecution. When you have nothing, you aren't afraid of losing anything. When you have died with Christ, you are not afraid of losing your life. When you suffer the pain of the cross willingly, pain has no grip on you through fear. As John says, "Love casts out all fear." And Paul says, "Death, where is thy sting?" This refers not only to the reward of life eternal but also to the here and now.

Are we realizing the promises of the kingdom today? If we are not, perhaps we have not yet really sacrificed. If we are not seeing communal growth, perhaps we have not really brought all of our private wealth to the cross. If we are not really at peace in our poverty, perhaps we are not yet really poor. Likewise, if we are not experiencing some persecution, perhaps our life is simply not challenging to anyone. Challenge evokes response. Response will bring both blessing and persecution. How we deal with both is an indication of how much we have really sacrificed.   □

Is God Fair?
Matthew 20:1-16 (20:Wednesday)

They complained to the owner. "This last group did only an hour's work, but you have put them on the same basis as us who have worked a full day in the scorching heat." "My friend," he said to one in reply, "I do you no injustice. . . . I intend to give this man who was hired last the same pay as you. I am free to do as I please with my money, am I not?" (v. 11-15)

So it is with God's justice. Just when we with our human deliberations think we have peace and social justice all figured out, God steps in and confuses the issue! God looks at justice from an eternal perspective. Our perspective is human and therefore quite limited. Sometimes God's justice appears unjust. Sometimes God seems to punish that which appears just. As Scripture says, "His ways are not your ways."

We can look at the example of King Saul. Before a battle Samuel promised Saul that he would come and offer sacrifice and invoke the blessing of God. When Samuel did not arrive at the agreed time, Saul said, "Now the Philistines will come down against me at Gilgal, and I have not yet sought the Lord's blessing." So he went ahead and offered the holocaust himself.

Some would think that Samuel was at fault for his lateness and that Saul acted righteously in at least seeking God through sacrifice and prayer. But no! God said to Saul through his prophet Samuel, "You have been foolish! Had you kept the command the Lord your God gave you, the Lord would now establish your kingship in Israel as lasting; but as things are, your kingdom shall not endure."

Likewise, Saul was commanded by God, "Go and put the sinful

Amalekites under a ban of destruction. Fight against them until you have exterminated them." Saul saved the sheep and oxen of the Amalekites to sacrifice in thanksgiving to God. Yet God said to Saul through Samuel, "Why then have you disobeyed the Lord? Does the Lord delight in holocaust and sacrifices as in obedience to the command of the Lord? Obedience is better than sacrifice. You rejected the command of the Lord and the Lord rejects you as king of Israel." It would seem Saul would be honored for wanting to thank God. But he was rebuked for presuming to guess the will of God. From a human perspective God's justice sometimes does seem a bit unjust.

Concerning God's election of some and his rejection of others Paul argues, "God has mercy on whom he wishes, and whom he wishes he makes obdurate. You will say to me, 'Why, then, does he find fault? For who can oppose his will?'. . . Does something molded say to its molder, 'Why did you made me like this?' Does not a potter have the right to make from the same lump of clay one vessel for a lofty purpose and another for a humble one? What if God, wishing to show his wrath and make known his power, has endured with much patience vessels fit for wrath, ready to be destroyed, and in order to make known the riches of his glory toward the vessels for mercy, which he prepared for glory—I am speaking about us whom he called." This is hard reasoning to endure. It is true God might "wish that all might be saved," but he knows that all will not, and in his omnipotence he ultimately controls this destiny in eternal justice.

Who are we to argue with God? Do we not believe that "God is love"? Do we not believe that "all things work together for the good of those who have been called according to his decree"? Then we must trust in his judgments. No, they might not always appear to be just by our limited judgment. But from God's eternal perspective all creation unfolds in the justification wrought by Christ. God's wisdom and love are infinite; ours is finite at best. Let us trust in his justice and serve him in humble obedience to his word. Then we will discover true peace and justice. ☐

The Simple Way
Matthew 22:1-14 (20:Thursday)

You must go out into the byroads and invite to the wedding anyone you come upon. . . . The invited are many, the elect are few. (v. 9, 14)

So often we want to choose only the people we like for our Christian communities, rather than those whom God is calling. We choose the talented, the gifted, and the good-looking. Jesus chose the lowborn to be his apostles. Simple fishermen and others of the working class constituted most of his apostles. Scholars speculate that only Judas was really well-educated, and he was the one who betrayed Jesus! No doubt we would have chosen a much better equipped band to follow us, were we the Messiah.

The Acts of the Apostles depicts Peter before the educated religious sophisticates of his day. It is said, "Observing the self-assurance of Peter and John, and realizing that the speakers were uneducated men of no standing, the questioners were amazed." Paul says of the first believers in Corinth, "Consider your situation. Not many of you are wise, as men account wisdom; not many are influential; and surely not many are well-born. God chose those whom the world considers absurd to shame the wise; he singled out the weak of this world to shame the strong. He chose the world's lowborn and despised, those who count for nothing, to reduce to nothing those who were something." He says conversely, "If any one of you thinks he is wise in a worldly way, he had better become a fool."

This does not mean we are not expected to appreciate God's gifts and grow in wisdom and holiness. In today's parable Jesus says of the one who came to the wedding feast not properly dressed, "Bind him hand and foot and throw him out into the night to wail and grind his teeth." We must truly reverence God's gift of salvation to us, the lowborn.

Likewise, we must be willing to grow in wisdom. Paul says to the church in Corinth, "I could not talk to you as spiritual men, but only as men of flesh, as infants in Christ." But to the Hebrews, "Let us, then, go beyond the initial teaching about Christ and advance to maturity." Sirach says of the person who studies the law of the Most High, "He is in attendance on the great and has entrance to the ruler. Many will praise his understanding, his fame can never be effaced." No doubt, even the simple and lowborn can become great saints and wise men and women in Christ.

Do we limit God's choice of his disciples to our own human consideration? Do we grow as a result of being rooted in Christ, or do we actually grow away from the simple teachings of Christ? Real wisdom begins in simplicity. □

No Greater Love
Matthew 22:34-40 (20:Friday)

On these two commandments the whole law is based, and the prophets as well. (v. 40)

Such simplicity. Such profound beauty! We study for years on end, poring over theological treatises and philosophical works to find the true meaning of life. We study the law and the prophets, reading page upon page, until our eyes fail and the lines begin to blur. Yet the meaning is so clear and simple that even the least literate of believers can understand.

"God is love, and he who abides in love abides in God, and God in him." This is a tall order! We must love with our whole heart and soul. We must direct our thoughts toward love. We must love in such a way as to involve God and our neighbor as much, if not more, than we love ourselves. So simple, yet forever challenging.

This theology is mystical and experiential. It is learned in the classroom of daily life, rather than in a seminary lecture hall. It is learned among the poor, rather than in the ivory towers of the religious rich.

The master of this class is Jesus Christ himself. "No greater love has any man than that he lay down his life for his friends." Jesus teaches us of this love on the cross. He teaches more by example than by words. Thus he becomes more than cold, empty words on a page; he becomes the living Word. This Word is clearly understood by those with an open heart of love.

How familiar are the sounds of these words of Scripture, yet how difficult they are to actually live! It is so much easier to be "religious"—to become involved in a particular approach to prayer, or to champion a particular issue, or to get involved in one or the other of the movements in the church. In themselves all of these are fine, yet without love none of them amounts to anything.

As Paul says in the famous thirteenth chapter of his first letter to the Corinthians, "If I speak with human tongues and angelic as well, but do not have love, I am a noisy gong, and clanging cymbal. If I have the gift of prophecy and, with full knowledge, comprehend all mysteries, if I have faith enough to move mountains, but have not love, I am nothing. If I give everything I have to feed the poor and hand over my body to be burned, but have not love, I gain nothing."

How similar are these words of Paul to the words of Christ: "Many will plead with me, 'Lord, Lord, have we not prophesied in your name? Have we not exorcised demons by its power? Did we not work many miracles in your name as well?' Then I will declare to them solemnly, 'I never knew you. Out of my sight, you evildoers!'" We must know Christ if we are to know love, and we must love if we are to truly please God. As John says, "God is love."

But what is the test of love? Jesus says, "No greater love has any man than this: that he should lay down his life for his friends." As Paul says, "It is rare that anyone should lay down his life for a just man, though it is barely possible that for a good man someone may have the courage to die. It is precisely in this that God proves his love for us: that while we were still sinners, Christ died for us."

Jesus tells us, "God so loved the world that he gave his only Son." The cross of Jesus is the ultimate expression of love: to die so that another might live—the righteous for the unrighteous, the rich for the poor, the strong to become ultimately weak so that the weak may be made strong. This is the power of the cross.

As Paul says, "I wish to know the power flowing from his resurrection; likewise to know how to share in his sufferings by being formed into the pattern of his death." You cannot know resurrection without the cross, for you cannot know new life without love, and you cannot know love without death to self. As Paul says, "Love is not self-seeking."

Do we seek ourselves in our expression of faith? If we do, then we do not really have the true faith. You cannot separate faith and love. If you do, you destroy them both! □

Dissent with Respect
Matthew 23:1-12 (20:Saturday)

The scribes and the Pharisees have succeeded Moses as teachers; therefore, do everything and observe everything they tell you. But do not follow their example. (v. 2-3)

Jesus recognized the offices of those in authority, and he submitted to that authority even unto death. But he also recognized the Jewish leaders' hypocrisy. He repeatedly warned against their personal sins.

Even the outspoken Paul recognized the authority of the Jewish leaders of his day. When he was struck on the mouth by the high priest's attendant, Paul said with typical resilience, "You are the one God will strike, you whitewashed wall! You sit there judging men according to the law, yet you violate the law yourself by ordering me to be struck." When the attendant said, "How dare you insult God's high priest?" Paul meekly responded, "My brothers, I did not know that he was the high priest. Indeed, Scripture has it, 'You shall not curse a prince of your people.'" Paul was respectful of this authority, even though he obviously had a rather low opinion of the high priest's personal holiness and justice.

Paul also had a high regard for authority in the church. He submitted the gospel he had received "by revelation" to the other apostles' authority, "to make sure the course I was pursuing, or had pursued, was not useless." Yet, though he respected Peter's authority in the church, "When Cephas came to Antioch I directly withstood him, because he was clearly in the wrong." Thus we get a clear example from Scripture on how God keeps the church from error regarding major doctrines of the faith. By God's grace this has always been done.

So did St. Francis approach authority within religious communities. "If a superior commands his subject anything that is against his conscience, the subject should not spurn his authority, even though he cannot obey him." Likewise, if a superior was bad for the community, "they who have the power to elect must elect someone else as minister general." This could only be done "if at any time it becomes clear to all the provincial ministers and custodes that the minister general is incapable of serving the friars and can be of no benefit to them." Yet in all cases authority must be properly respected, for as Paul says, "There is no authority except from God."

This does not keep Jesus from pronouncing his disdain of the personal example of the scribes and Pharisees: "Their words are bold but their deeds are few. They bind up heavy loads, hard to carry, to lay on other men's shoulders, while they themselves will not lift a finger to bridge them. All their works are performed to be seen." It appears that the curse of "religiosity" is not unique to our time. Jesus dealt with it too and roundly condemned it.

How do we deal with hypocrisy among clergy and religious? Speak out? Yes, we must, but always with humble respect. Most importantly we speak by our own holiness. As Jesus says, "Unless your holiness surpasses that of the scribes and Pharisees you shall not enter the kingdom of God." Does our own holiness surpass that of the clergy and religious we so freely criticize? We are probably equal before God when it comes to sin, for "all have sinned and fallen short of the glory of God." Awareness of our sin should make us all more merciful toward one another. This is the first step toward real holiness. □

The Pharisee within Us
Matthew 23:13-22 (21:Monday)

Woe to you scribes and Pharisees, you frauds! (v. 13)

How frightening are the words of Jesus to the scribes and Pharisees! They hit too close to home to allow us to feel comfortable. There is still a little of the scribe and the Pharisee living within our own hearts.

We preach the kingdom of God, but rarely do we take the time to enter into it ourselves. We travel the world to evangelize the nations, while Christians in our own nation support foreign policies and affluent life-styles that oppress and even kill the poor and downtrodden of the world. We build religious systems and associations of men, adding line upon line and precept upon precept, often making it difficult for the common person to experience the simple gospel of Jesus Christ.

Yes, we shut the door of the kingdom of God to ourselves and others in many ways, all the while doing so in the name of our Lord and Savior Jesus Christ. Surely we must heed Jesus' words that even the whores and prostitutes will enter into the kingdom before we do.

We must allow Jesus to forgive and change the scribe and the Pharisee within our own hearts. We must look now to the "weightier matters of the law, justice and mercy and good faith," knowing that all the commandments of true religion are fulfilled in Jesus' royal law of love. Once we return to this simple gospel of love, we will find we have fulfilled all the rest.

We must allow our hearts to be wounded toward the poor and the afflicted, then we will cease wounding others in the name of religion. □

Cleanse the Inside
Matthew 23:23-26 (21:Tuesday)

Woe to you scribes and Pharisees, you frauds! You cleanse the outside of cup and dish, and leave the inside filled with loot and lust! Blind Pharisee! First cleanse the inside of the cup so that its outside may be clean. (v. 25-26)

So often we externalize our "renewal in the Spirit." We argue about external forms of prayer without really entering into prayer. We expend all our available energy on how to pray, so we have little time or energy left to actually pray. We crusade around the world encouraging people to worship, but rarely do we ourselves worship.

The same is true of some radical gospel communities. We have meeting after meeting to discuss radical gospel life-styles; we amass line upon line of constitutions, statutes, and church decrees describing this radical call to follow Jesus. Yet when it comes to actually doing it, we have little time or energy left over. We have become a religious people who talk much of peace, poverty, and prayer but still have unrest and greed in our hearts because we seldom take time to actually pray and be alone with Jesus.

It is said of Jesus, "He often retired to deserted places and prayed." He taught his disciples that private prayer is important: "Whenever you pray, go to your room, close the door, and pray to your Father in private." Granted, as a Jew he prayed the liturgy and celebrated the feast days of the Jews; the Eucharist was in fact instituted during the Passover. But Jesus emphasized deep and sincere internal prayer.

Paul also teaches a faith that is primarily internal. As he says to the Galatians, "Now that you have come to know God—or rather, have been known by him—how can you return to those powerless, worthless, natural elements to which you seem willing to enslave yourselves once more? You even go so far as to keep the ceremonial observance of days and months, seasons and years! I fear for you; all my efforts with you may have been wasted." Granted, Paul is speaking primarily of a return to Judaism, which required such things as circumcision, and to paganism, which was often simple idolatry. But the same fears can be applied to our own Christian liturgy. We can become so preoccupied with even proper externals that we end up in error.

How often has the Lord's Prayer been but a repetition of words? Yet Jesus said in instituting this prayer, "In your prayer do not rattle on like the pagans. They think they will win a hearing by the sheer multiplication of words. Do not imitate them. Your Father knows what you need before you ask him." Ironically, we often pray this prayer in direct opposition to the intention for which it was taught. We do the same with many of our rules and regulations regarding both communal life and liturgical prayer.

Cleansing the outside of the dish first is useless; we must first cleanse the inside. The inside is more important, for it holds the food and drink that bring either healthy nourishment or filth and disease to our bodies. We must cleanse the inside of the dish through repentance and prayer if we are to really give living water and the Bread of Life to a hungry and dying world. □

Don't Murder Your Prophets!
Matthew 23:27-32 (21:Wednesday)

You say, "Had we lived in our forefathers' time we would not have joined them in shedding the prophets' blood." Thus you show you are the sons of the prophets' murderers. Now it is your turn: fill up the vessel measured out by your forefathers. (v. 30-32)

Do we build tombs and monuments for the prophets and saints, only to kill those of our own day and time by our indifference? We honor various saints of the past, but do we really heed their words, much less listen to the saints of our own day? We fill our calendars with saints' days and dot the countryside with religious shrines, but do our lives reflect their examples?

St. Francis says we love to quote the sayings of the saints but do not like to do what they say. If we are really to honor the prophets and the saints, we should rend our hearts and radically reform our lives. If we quote their words, we should also imitate their Christ-like lives.

Jesus says the "religious" of the future will not listen any better than did the murderers of the prophets—or those who crucified him! "I shall send you prophets and wise men and scribes. Some you will kill and crucify, others you will flog in your synagogues and hunt down from city to city." How often these words have been true even within Christianity! Protestants and Catholics have persecuted one another. Even the Franciscans used to hunt down and persecute various reformers who were the instruments of the Spirit to start great movements of renewal.

Then there are the saints and prophets of our own time—the untold few who have no place on our calendars, no churches or shrines bearing their names, yet whose names are written in heaven. Do we hear them? Jesus says the "religious" people will persecute and kill the prophets he sends. Do we put a knife through their hearts by our indifference? Oh yes, they are fun to listen to at prayer meetings, conferences, and social gatherings; but do we really heed their words any more than we have heeded the prophets of old? As the prophet Ezekiel says, "For them you are only a ballad singer with a pleasant voice and a clever touch. They listen to your words, but they will not obey them."

We can gain wisdom on how to approach the renewal groups and prophets of our own time by observing the attitude of one Jewish teacher during the time of the apostles. Gamaliel, you will recall, was Paul's teacher, for Paul said, "I sat at the feet of Gamaliel and was educated strictly in the law of our fathers." When the Sanhedrin was set on silencing the followers of Jesus, Gamaliel said, "Let them alone. If their purpose or activity is human in its origins, it will destroy itself. If, on the other hand, it comes from God, you will not be able to destroy them without fighting against God himself."

Granted, there is need for discipline and authority in the church. Paul said, "There are many irresponsible teachers—men who are empty talkers and deceivers. These must be silenced." But Paul told Timothy to fight by "preaching the word, staying with this task whether convenient or inconvenient—correcting, reproving, appealing—constantly teaching and never losing patience." Let us carefully discern who are the true prophets, teachers, and saints of our time. Then let us heed their words and follow their example. □

Preparing for the End
Matthew 24:42-51 (21:Thursday)

Stay awake, therefore! You cannot know the day your Lord is coming. . . . Happy that servant whom his master discovers at work on his return! (v. 42, 46)

We are only ready to go if we are ready to stay, and we are only ready to stay if we are ready to go! Today's gospel tells us to live every day as if it were the day of the Lord's coming. But this should not make us lazy; it should make us work all the harder. We should live every day as if it were our last, getting the most we can out of each day for the kingdom of Christ.

Paul says, "Awake, O sleeper, arise from the dead, and Christ will give you light. . . . Make the most of the present opportunity, for these are evil days." He also says to the Thessalonians, "You are not in the dark, brothers, that the day should catch you off guard, like a thief. No, all of you are children of light and of the day. We belong neither to darkness nor to night; therefore let u not be asleep like the rest, but awake and sober! ... We who live by day must be alert, putting on faith and love as a breastplate and the hope of salvation as a helmet."

Being always alert in waiting for the coming of Christ makes us very effective in living out God's plan for holiness on the face of this earth. Paul spoke about the question of the Lord's coming, which had frightened some and caused them to totally abandon their responsibilities: "On the question of the coming of our Lord Jesus Christ and our being gathered to him, we beg you, brothers, not to be so easily agitated or terrified. ... We hear that some of you are unruly, not keeping busy but acting like busybodies. We enjoin all such ... to earn the food they eat by working quietly. You must not grow weary of doing what is right, brothers." As he says in his first letter to the Thessalonians, "Make it a point of honor to remain at peace and attend to your own affairs. Work with your hands as we directed you to do, so that you will give good example to outsiders and want for nothing."

Paul speaks similarly regarding holiness in sexual morality. Jesus might rightly say, "When people rise from the dead, they neither marry nor are given in marriage, but live like angels in heaven." But this does not mean sexuality is no longer important. Paul says to the end-times-conscious Thessalonians, "It is God's will that you grow in holiness: that you abstain from immorality, each of you guarding his member in sanctity and honor, not in passionate desire as do the Gentiles."

Returning to our duty to live in daylight he says, "Light produces every kind of goodness and justice and truth. Be correct in your judgment of what pleases the Lord. Take no part in vain deeds done in darkness; rather, condemn them. It is shameful even to mention the things these people do in secret."

Do we sometimes say, "What the hell? Its all gonna' burn anyhow?" Do we stop trying just because it seems so futile to try and end the evil in this world? Granted, Peter in his second letter says, "The day of the Lord will come like a thief. ... The heavens will be destroyed in flames and the elements will melt away in a blaze." But he also says, "While waiting for this, make every effort to be found without stain or defilement, and at peace in his sight." The teaching of the second coming of Jesus should not frighten

us nor lead us to give in to the world in despair. Rather it should prompt us to work all the more.

Paul says, "Thenceforth, we shall be with the Lord unceasingly. Console one another with this message. . . . Therefore, comfort and upbuild one another." We must get busy in comforting and upbuilding. There is much to do on earth, for the time is short. After that we will be forever in "a new heaven and a new earth where, according to his promise, the justice of God will reside." ☐

Keep Your Light Burning
Matthew 25:1-13 (21:Friday)

The reign of God can be likened to ten bridesmaids who took their torches and went out to welcome the groom. Five of them were foolish, while the other five were sensible. (v. 1-2)

I have often wondered if the sensible virgins were not a little selfish in not sharing their oil with the foolish ones. Shouldn't they have done with less so that their friends could have had just a little?

However, we cannot think in these terms when referring to the "oil" of the Spirit. We can certainly pray for others. We can say with Paul, "I could even wish to be separated from Christ for the sake of my brothers." But we cannot take part of the anointing of the Holy Spirit given to us and give it to others. That is a matter left to the free working of God's grace.

If anything, we should be "selfish" when seeking the Spirit of God. As the writer of the classic book of prayer *The Cloud of Unknowing* says, "We should be moderate in all things but prayer." And the author of *The Hermitage Within* says, "We have the right to covet but one thing. . . . We can be greedy for the good." We need to zealously seek the grace of the Spirit, drinking in as much as we can possibly hold. Then we can overflow into the desert of this world and help turn the parched land into living springs.

Make no mistake about it: The oil for the lamp of our life with Christ is the Holy Spirit. We must fill our life with the Spirit every day if we are to be the light of the world. We cannot be passive in this endeavor; we must actively "fan into full flame" the gift we have received. This gift from God is the Holy Spirit.

We cannot assume that Jesus will delay his second coming. Today could very well be the day. We should live every day as if it were our last. If we are always ready to go and be with Jesus, then we are ready to stay. If we are ready to stay and meet the challenge of this world by living the gospel without compromise, then we are ready to go.

Would we really want Jesus to come back, only to find us not really "burning brightly" in the fire of love that comes from the Holy Spirit of God? We must actually fill our lamps with oil through zealous and charismatic prayer, so the fire of our life with Christ might burn brightly and shine divine light into the darkness of this world. Then we will be ever ready to gaze upon the face of Christ when he comes again. ☐

Building Spiritual Muscles
Matthew 25:14-30 (21:Saturday)

Those who have will get more until they grow rich, while those who have not will lose even the little they have. (v. 29)

What do we do with the gifts God gives us? Do we really use them to their full potential, or do we use them only halfway?

This does not necessarily mean we must go out and build big ministries for Jesus. It means we must be fully committed, radical Christians. We must be "lean and mean" Christians. Have we grown fat and lazy? American Christianity tends to propagate a gospel that says, "Big is better," While Jesus tells us that only if we are faithful in the little things will we be given more. We must go after the one stray sheep instead of only looking for the big flock. Jesus is interested in personal solutions. He is not corporate-minded like an IBM or an AT&T. He is Jesus, our personal Savior.

Mother Teresa of Calcutta is a woman who has used her gifts and talents in this radical way. She began with only five *rupees* in her pocket, but she had a "heart of gold." She dared to care for the poorest of the poor. She went from person to person, individual to individual, sharing the riches of our poor Savior Jesus Christ. She went forth with no greater plan, no greater talent, than to care. Because of this, God has made hers a powerful voice in the world.

We must never quench the Spirit or stifle the gifts; we must let the gifts prosper. Spiritual gifts are like muscles: the more you use them, the stronger they become. Have we taken these gifts for granted and grown fat and flabby?

I recall here the balance of St. Francis and his first companions. The charismatics of today have yet to see a Pentecostal outpouring of the Spirit as free as theirs. Raptures, ecstasies, tongues, words of knowledge, prophecies, and healings were all common experiences among the first Franciscans. At the same time they served the lepers and the poor in a way that certainly exceeds our efforts, taking the time to lovingly and carefully wash their sores and "bind up their wounds." As one of my Franciscan brothers noted of a shut-in he recently visited, "The man was impressed most by the simple fact that we just had the time to talk to him." In all this we must remain little brothers, willing to become poor in order to bring the riches of the kingdom of God to the poor of the world.

We are called today to expand in this littleness. We must break with the "big is better" mentality of the Western world and learn the foolishness of the cross of Jesus, which says, "Small is beautiful." We must courageously open ourselves to the full outpouring of the Holy Spirit, or else we will not increase the gifts of God in our life. We must be willing to become truly poor in order to bring the good news to the poor. If we are not willing to "go for it," we will never increase the gifts Jesus has given us to share with the whole world. If we are not willing to get radical for Christ, Jesus will never be a radical force in our lives, and we will remain in our darkness and pain. □

Another Book of Interest

Reflections on the Gospels
Volume One
John Michael Talbot

"People who undertake scripture reading for the first time can be often overwhelmed by the sheer volume of words, from the first phrase in Genesis to the last period in Revelation. In *Reflections on the Gospels*, John Michael Talbot has done such readers an invaluable Christian service. His meditations are concise and demanding to the point. Short, crisp sentences command our attention, provoke us to thought."—Bruce Ritter, O.F.M. Conv. Founder, Covenant House. $5.95